WUTHERING HEIGHTS

by
Emily Brontë

Student Packet

Written by:
Mary L. Dennis
Karen Brookwell-Miller

Contains masters for:

1	Prereading Activity
6	Vocabulary Activities
1	Study Guide (five pages)
3	Literary Analysis Activities
5	Critical Thinking Activities
1	Creative Writing Activity
1	Review Activity
1	Vocabulary Quiz
2	Comprehension Quizzes
2	Unit Exams (two levels)

PLUS Detailed Answer Key

Note

The text used to prepare this guide was the Bantam Classic softcover edition published in March, © 1981. *Wuthering Heights* was fist published in 1847. The page references may differ in the hardcover or other paperback editions.

ISBN 1-56137-460-1

©1999 Novel Units, Inc. All rights reserved. Printed in the United States of America. Limited reproduction permission: The publisher grants permission to individual teachers who have purchased this book, or for whom it has been purchased, to reproduce the blackline masters as needed for use with their own students. Reproduction for an entire school or school district or for commercial use is prohibited.

To order, contact your local school supply store, or—

Novel Units, Inc.
P.O. Box 791610
San Antonio, TX 78279

Name_____

Wuthering Heights
Activity #1: Anticipation Guide
Use Before Reading

Anticipation Guide

Write "A" next to statements with which you agree. If you disagree, write "D." If you're not sure, write "NS." After you have read the novel, look at your answers again and see if you want to change any of them.

_____ 1. True love is forever—once you are in love with someone, no one else will do.

_____ 2. Sometimes, a slow steady fire is better than a raging inferno.

_____ 3. The worst thing about a broken heart is that it keeps beating.

_____ 4. Love and romance are the same thing.

_____ 5. "All you need is love." (The Beatles)

_____ 6. Success is the best revenge.

_____ 7. The taste of revenge is always sweet.

_____ 8. "Conscience is born of love." (Shakespeare)

_____ 9. If a person is born into a certain social class, he or she should marry within that class.

_____ 10. When women marry, they should give all of their property and money to their husbands.

_____ 11. Marrying one's cousin can be financially advantageous.

_____ 12. If you are truly in love, death cannot separate you spiritually.

_____ 13. There is a difference between love and obsession.

_____ 14. "It lies not in our power to love or hate
For will in us is overruled by fate." (Christopher Marlowe)

_____ 15. People who have had few advantages should be forgiven for their actions, no matter how cruel.

© Novel Units, Inc.   All rights reserved

Name_____

Wuthering Heights
Activity #2: Vocabulary
Chapters I-VI

Group Vocabulary Activity

A task like finding the meanings for a long list of words can be much easier and more enjoyable when everyone pitches in.
1. Form four groups. Each group is in charge of the words on one of the lists below.
2. Divide the words in your group's list so that each group member has one or two words. Make word maps for your word(s), using the format below.
3. Meet quietly with your group, sharing your word maps.
4. Choose a representative or two to share your group's words with the class.

Word Lists: (Page numbers where words are found follow the words.)

Group #1	Group #2	Group #3	Group #4
misanthropist 1	soliloquised 2	penetralium 2	sundry 3
impertinence 3	tacit 4	physiognomy 5	dispatch 5
prudential 6	laconic 6	churlish 7	assiduity 9
sagacity 9	taciturn 10	miscreants 15	vapid 16
asseverated 18	lachrymose 18	querulous 25	vindictive 35
curate 36	vociferated 43	culpable 44	execrations 44

Word Map Format:

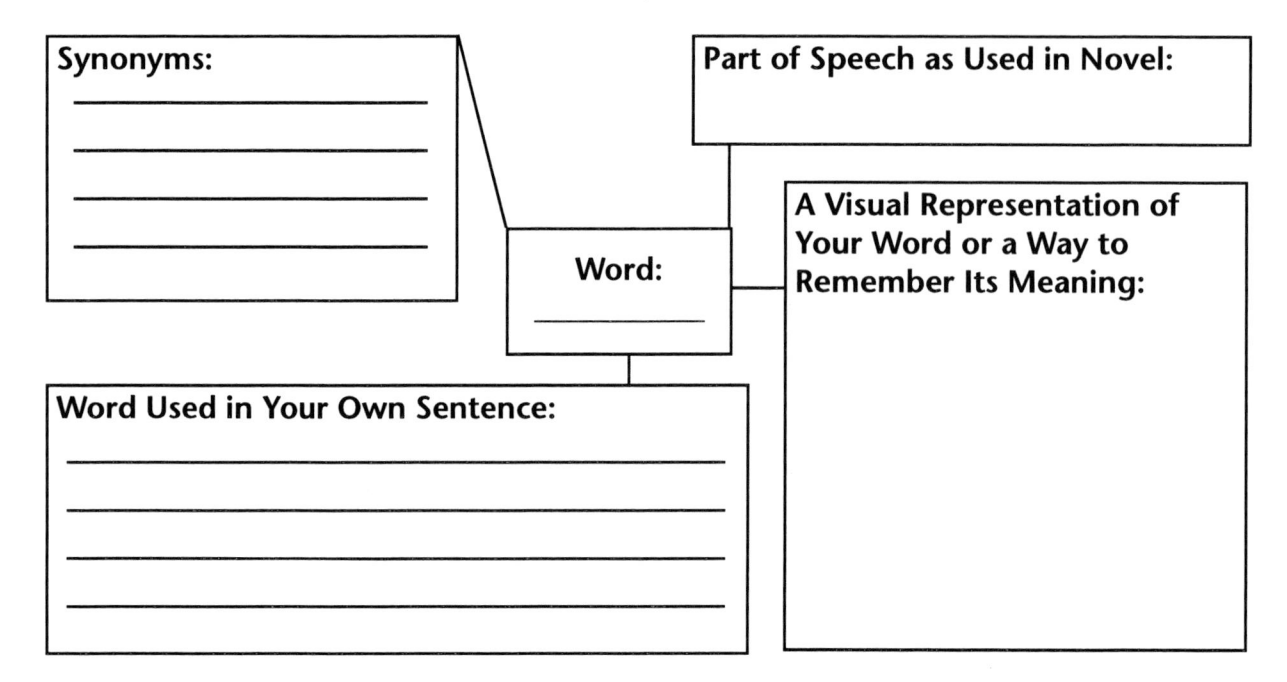

Synonyms:	Part of Speech as Used in Novel:
Word:	A Visual Representation of Your Word or a Way to Remember Its Meaning:
Word Used in Your Own Sentence:	

© Novel Units, Inc. All rights reserved

Name_____

Wuthering Heights
Activity #3: Vocabulary
Chapters VII-XII

blackguard 47	expostulated 52	cambric 53	equanimity 53
prognosticate 55	consumption 57	dissipation 59	petulantly 62
consternation 64	vociferating 66	vagaries 66	winsome 70
munificent 81	dilatory 82	sizar 82	protract 88
abjured 91	avarice 94	mitigating 97	propitiate 100
approbation 102	compunction 108	pertinaciously 109	deranged 111
paroxysm 115	recantation 118	scruple 119	sovereign 121

Directions: From the list above, find a synonym for each word or definition below and write it on the line. All the words will not be used.

1. stability, evenness of temper _____
2. intemperance _____
3. villain _____
4. hesitation or sense of regret _____
5. principle _____
6. spasm _____
7. greed _____
8. insane _____
9. slow _____
10. gold coin _____
11. foretell _____
12. conciliate _____
13. lengthen _____
14. generous _____
15. tuberculosis _____

© Novel Units, Inc.

All rights reserved

Name_____

Wuthering Heights
Activity #4: Vocabulary
Chapters XIII-XVIII

ACROSS
2. vengeful threats
6. like the Devil
7. shining; brilliant
9. tranquility
12. name (thing or person)
13. heretical
15. slovenly woman
16. hopeless
18. dull and uninteresting
19. gate or window
20. toll for making meal
21. dreary (colloquial)
22. boldness

DOWN
1. repeated statement
3. restlessness
4. make unnecessary
5. willingness
8. depression; hopelessness
10. begged
11. imperious
14. cheerful
17. horrible; reprehensible

---

diabolical
iteration
abject
scintillating
quiescence
magisterial
thible
heterodox
comminations
disquietude
obviate
slattern
audacity
odious
importuned
insipid
alacrity
appellation
despondency
sanquine
dree
wicket

© Novel Units, Inc.　　　　　　　　All rights reserved

Name_____

Wuthering Heights
Activity #5: Vocabulary
Chapters XIX-XXIV

incipient 184	trepidation 185	filial 191	salubrious 198
mortification 203	copious 207	epistle 208	immolation 210
Michaelmas 210	diurnal 210	tenure 211	expedient 213
elysium 217	pathos 220	usurped 224	undulating 227
discomfited 229	interdict 234		

Directions: Some simple sentences appear below. Use words from the list to expand them. Try to use three or more list words in each sentence; you may want to use different forms of the words (i.e. "mortified" instead of "mortification"). Underline the words from the list that you use in each sentence.

1. She wept. _____

2. He crept. _____

3. She ran. _____

4. He can. _____

5. He lied. _____

6. She died. _____

© Novel Units, Inc.   All rights reserved

Name_____

Wuthering Heights
Activity #6: Vocabulary
Chapters XXV-XXIX

Directions: In the sentences below, vocabulary words are underlined. Rewrite each sentence, without changing its meaning, so that it is clear you know the meaning of the underlined word.

Example: "…he harped on the cruel obligation of being held <u>asunder</u> from his friend and love…"
Rewritten: "…he repeated that it was cruel to keep him apart from his friend and love…"

1. "…the hollowness round them transforming to haggard wildness the <u>languid</u> expression they once possessed." (page 239)
   _____
   _____

2. "The havoc that months had previously wrought was now <u>emulated</u> by the inroads of hours." (page 242) _____
   _____

3. "…and her poor little heart <u>reproached</u> itself for even that passing forgetfulness of its cares." (page 243) _____
   _____

4. "…his cousin's patience was not sufficient to endure this <u>enigmatical</u> behaviour." (page 243) _____
   _____

5. "To the devil with your <u>clamour</u>!" (page 251) _____
   _____

6. "I seated myself in a chair, and rocked, to and fro, passing harsh judgement on my many <u>derelictions</u> of duty…" (page 253) _____
   _____

7. "I got the <u>sexton</u>, who was digging Linton's grave, to remove the earth off her coffin-lid…" (page 263)_____
   _____

© Novel Units, Inc.   All rights reserved

Name_____

Wuthering Heights
Activity #7: Vocabulary
Chapters XXX-XXXIV

fortnight 269	destitute 269	condescend 272	adroitly 273
smiting 281	retaliate 283	reproved 285	obdurate 287
paragon 289	disenchanted 294	monomania 296	
bane 301	vigilance 302		

Directions: Match each word from the list above with its etymology, below.

1. Latin: *de* (down) + *statuere* (to set) _____

2. French: *à* (to) + *droit* (right) _____

3. OE: *feowertene* (fourteen) + *nicht* (night) _____

4. OE: *bana* (killer) _____

5. Latin: *vigil* (awake) _____

6. OE: *smitan* (to strike) _____

7. Latin: *re* (back) + *talio* (punishment in kind) _____

8. Latin: *cum* (with) + *descendere* (to stoop) _____

9. Greek: *monos* (single) + *mania* (madness) _____

10. Latin: *ob* (against) + *durate* (harden) _____

11. Italian: *paragone* (touchstone) _____

12. Latin: *re* (again) + *probare* (to test) _____

13. Latin: *dis* (away from) + *in* (without) + *cantare* (to sing) _____

© Novel Units, Inc.　　　　　　　　　　　　　　　　　　　　　　All rights reserved

Name_____

Wuthering Heights
Study Guide

Directions: Answer each question briefly but completely. Use your completed study guide later on to study for quizzes and tests.

Chapters I-VI

1. What is the mood of the first chapter? If you were at Wuthering Heights, what sounds would you hear?
2. What is Mr. Heathcliff like? Does he seem very glad to see Lockwood?
3. What new characters are introduced in Chapter II? Are their identities made clear?
4. What sentence at the beginning of Chapter III is an example of foreshadowing?
5. What information does Lockwood learn that then becomes a part of his nightmare?
6. What is Heathcliff's reaction to Lockwood's nightmare?
7. What structural change occurs in the novel in Chapter IV?
8. How did Heathcliff breed bad feelings in the Earnshaw house?
9. What is Cathy Earnshaw like? Would you want her for a friend?
10. What are Hindley's feelings about Heathcliff?
11. What are Heathcliff's feelings about Hindley?
12. How do the lives of Cathy, Heathcliff, and Nelly change after Mr. Earnshaw's death?
13. Compare the reactions of the Lintons to Cathy and to Heathcliff.

Chapters VII-XII

14. How does Catherine change after her stay with the Lintons?
15. What conflict develops between Catherine and Heathcliff?
16. How does it happen that Nelly, a servant, is so well-spoken and intelligent?

© Novel Units, Inc.   All rights reserved

Name_____

Wuthering Heights
Study Guide • Page 2

17. How does his wife's death affect Hindley? Is he happy to be a father?

18. Who saves Hareton from death? Why is he immediately sorry?

19. What choice must Catherine make?

20. How might Catherine's marriage to Edgar help Heathcliff?

21. Does Catherine decide to marry Edgar because she loves him more than Heathcliff?

22. To what does Catherine compare her love for Edgar and her love for Heathcliff?

23. How does Heathcliff's departure indirectly bring tragedy?

24. How does Heathcliff's return bring emotional chaos?

25. What information does Nelly learn from Hareton?

26. What does Heathcliff now seem to be determined to accomplish?

27. What happens to Isabella's dog, Fanny? Who do you think is responsible?

28. How has Catherine reacted to Heathcliff's return and his subsequent fighting with Edgar and elopement with Isabella?

Chapters XIII-XVIII

29. How is Isabella received in her new home?

30. What different form does the narrative take in Chapter XIII?

31. How does Heathcliff perceive his love for Catherine in comparison to how he believes Edgar feels about her?

32. How does Heathcliff have Isabella legally in his control?

33. How does Catherine envision her afterlife?

34. Whose fault do you think it is that both Heathcliff's and Cathy's hearts are broken?

Name_____

Wuthering Heights
Study Guide • Page 3

35. Why did Edgar hope for a son?

36. What is Heathcliff's reaction to Catherine's death?

37. What does the change of weather (Chapter XVII) add to the mood?

38. What has happened to Hindley?

39. Explain Heathcliff's metaphor comparing Hareton to a tree (page 172).

40. How do we learn about what's been going on at Wuthering Heights?

41. Where does Isabella go? What happens there?

42. Describe young Catherine.

43. How does Catherine meet Hareton? What is her reaction to learning he is her cousin?

Chapters XIX-XXIV

44. How is Linton Heathcliff like/unlike his uncle?

45. What is Heathcliff's only interest in his son?

46. How long is it before Cathy sees her cousin Linton again?

47. How has Heathcliff used Hareton for his revenge on Hindley? How do they feel about one another?

48. What secret activity does Nelly learn about?

49. How does the end of her "romance" affect Cathy?

50. According to Heathcliff, how has the end of his contact with Cathy affected Linton?

51. If you were Cathy, how would you react to Linton? How does she?

52. How is Cathy able to see Linton in the evenings?

Name_____

Wuthering Heights
Study Guide • Page 4

53. What new insight do we get concerning Linton's personality and behavior?

54. When Cathy's visits are discovered, what compromise is reached?

Chapters XXV-XXIX

55. What is Edgar's situation?

56. What do Linton's letters to Edgar imply?

57. Why has Edgar decided it will be all right for Cathy to marry Linton?

58. Why does Linton insist he is feeling stronger? What do you think is really going on?

59. How does Linton turn out to be a traitor?

60. What does Heathcliff force Cathy to do?

61. What is Cathy's main reason for distress during the five days at the Heights?

62. How does Linton show he's not completely selfish?

63. Why is Heathcliff now master of Thrushcross Grange?

64. What did Heathcliff get the sexton to do?

65. What does Heathcliff want the sexton to do when he dies?

Chapters XXX-XXXIV

66. What was in Linton's will?

67. How has Cathy changed? Why?

68. Why does Cathy make fun of Hareton?

69. How much time passes between Chapters XXXI and XXXII?

Name_____

Wuthering Heights
Study Guide • Page 5

70. At the beginning of Chapter XXXII, how is positive change foreshadowed?

71. How did Heathcliff gradually disintegrate, while Hareton began to redeem himself?

72. Why did Heathcliff finally seem so happy?

73. To what do you attribute Heathcliff's illness and death?

74. At the end of the novel, which has proved to be the stronger force—love or hate?

Conclusions: In the space below, make notes about the possible themes of the novel, any symbolism you noted, and stylistic or structural characteristics which are notable.

Name_____

Wuthering Heights
Activity #8: Setting
Use During Reading

Directions: The novel takes place in two settings, Wuthering Heights and Thrushcross Grange. Each location has a different mood and feeling, yet there are likenesses as well. As you read, note the differences and likenesses of the two settings.

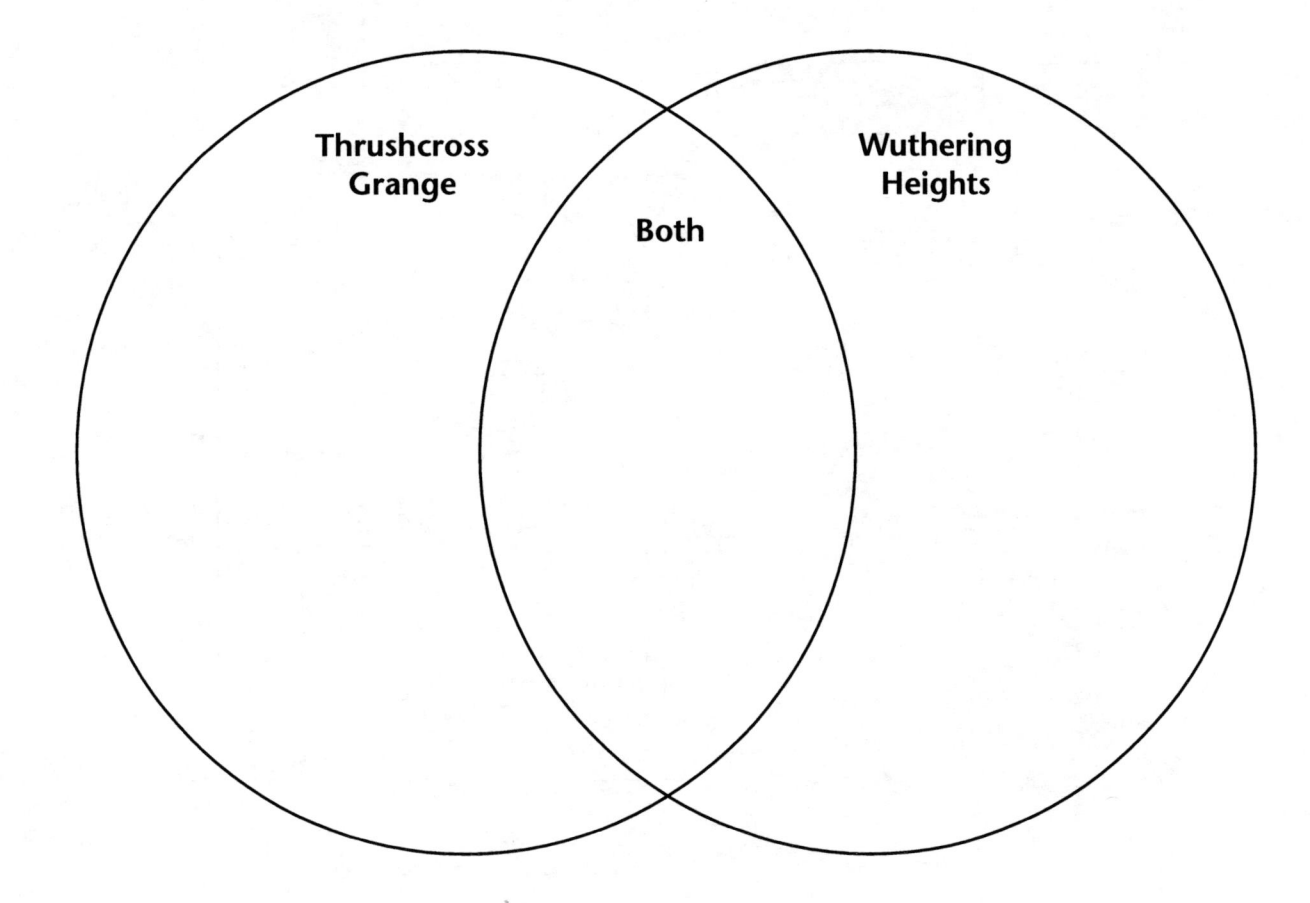

Thrushcross Grange — **Both** — **Wuthering Heights**

Name_____

Wuthering Heights
Activity #9: Critical Thinking
Use During Reading

Directions: When Emily Brontë wrote *Wuthering Heights,* she had to make sure her characters' ages coordinated with dates stated in the novel and with other mentions of time passing. If you are a **very observant** reader, you will be able to complete the chart below by the time you finish the novel.

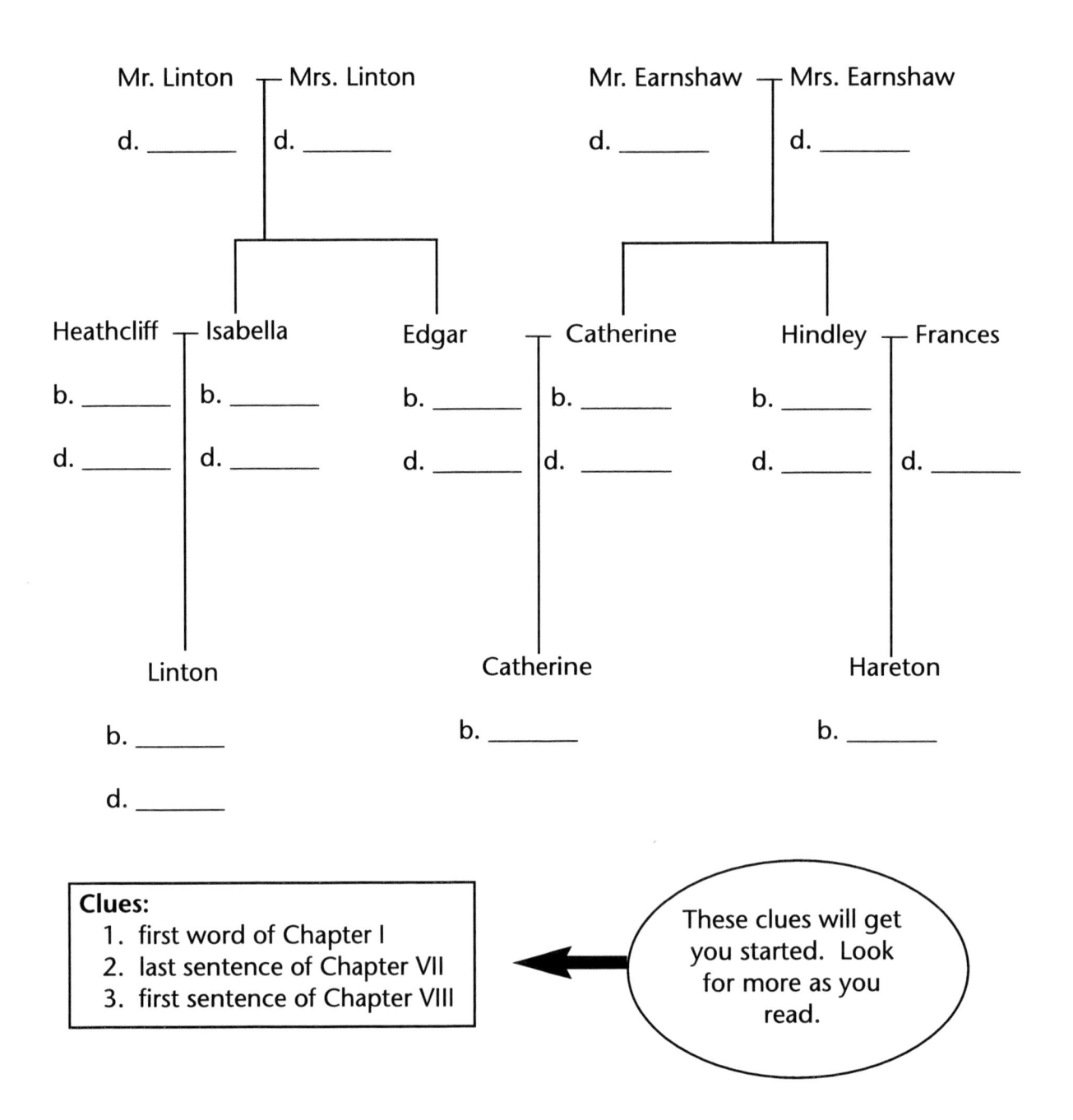

Mr. Linton — Mrs. Linton   Mr. Earnshaw — Mrs. Earnshaw
d. _____   d. _____   d. _____   d. _____

Heathcliff — Isabella   Edgar — Catherine   Hindley — Frances
b. _____ b. _____ b. _____ b. _____ b. _____
d. _____ d. _____ d. _____ d. _____ d. _____ d. _____

Linton   Catherine   Hareton
b. _____   b. _____   b. _____
d. _____

Clues:
1. first word of Chapter I
2. last sentence of Chapter VII
3. first sentence of Chapter VIII

These clues will get you started. Look for more as you read.

© Novel Units, Inc.   16   All rights reserved

Name_____

Wuthering Heights
Activity #10: Sociogram
Use During Reading

Directions: A sociogram is a way of tracking the way a character relates to others in the novel. In the diagram below, jot notes to indicate how Heathcliff feels about the characters around him, and how they in turn feel about him. Add to your diagram as you continue reading.

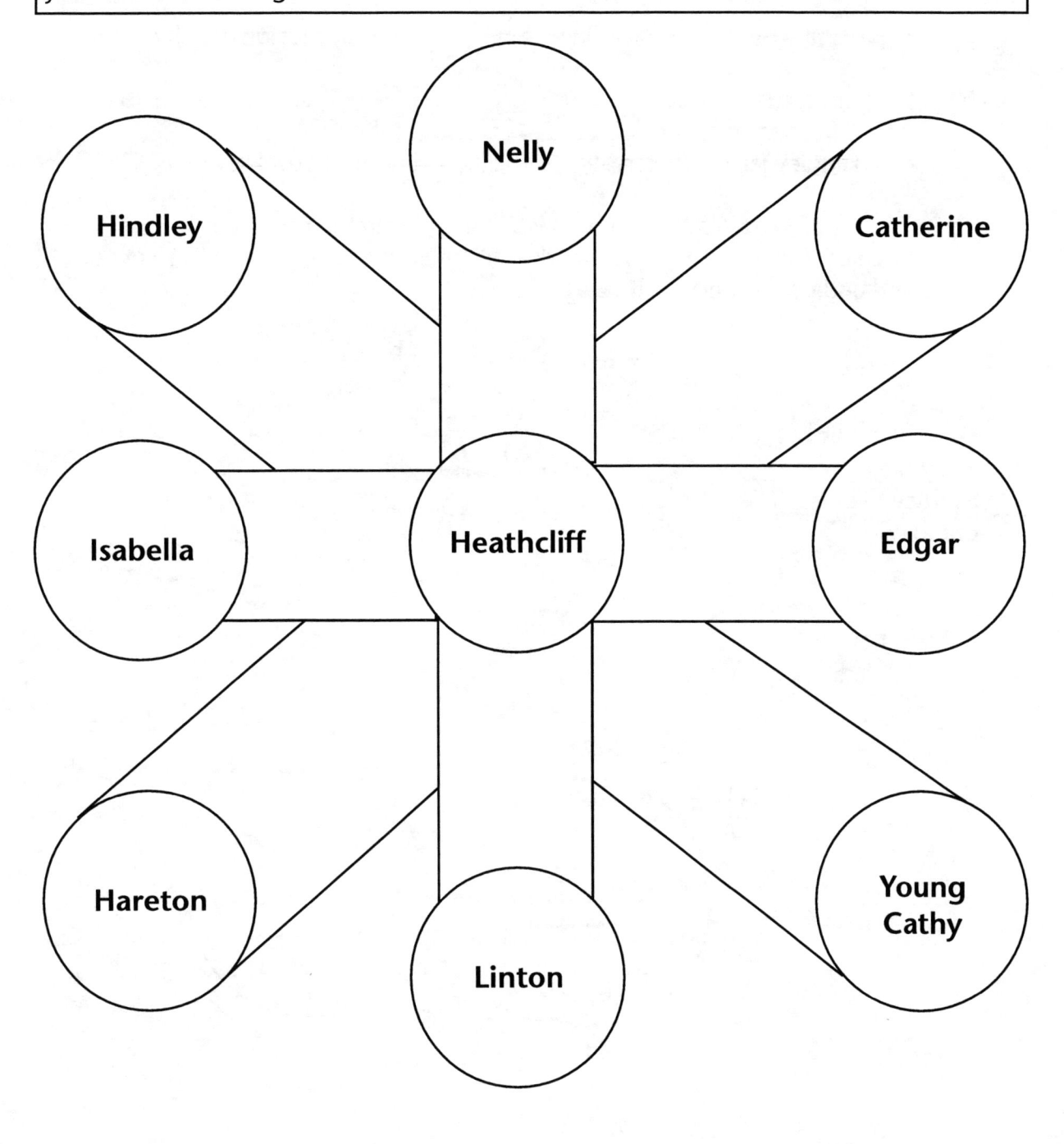

- Nelly
- Hindley
- Catherine
- Isabella
- Heathcliff
- Edgar
- Hareton
- Linton
- Young Cathy

© Novel Units, Inc. All rights reserved

Name_____

Wuthering Heights
Activity #11: Cause and Effect
Use After Reading

Directions: One event often results in another. The first is known as the cause and the second as the effect.

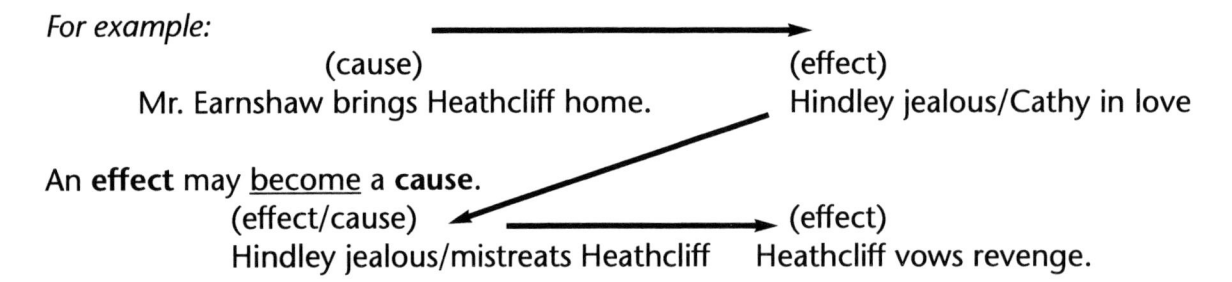

For example:

(cause) ⟶ (effect)
Mr. Earnshaw brings Heathcliff home.   Hindley jealous/Cathy in love

An **effect** may <u>become</u> a **cause**.

(effect/cause) ⟶ (effect)
Hindley jealous/mistreats Heathcliff   Heathcliff vows revenge.

Complete the cause-and-effect map below by filling in circles 2 through 7. The completed chart should show a chain of events, beginning with Heathcliff's vow of revenge and ending with his death.

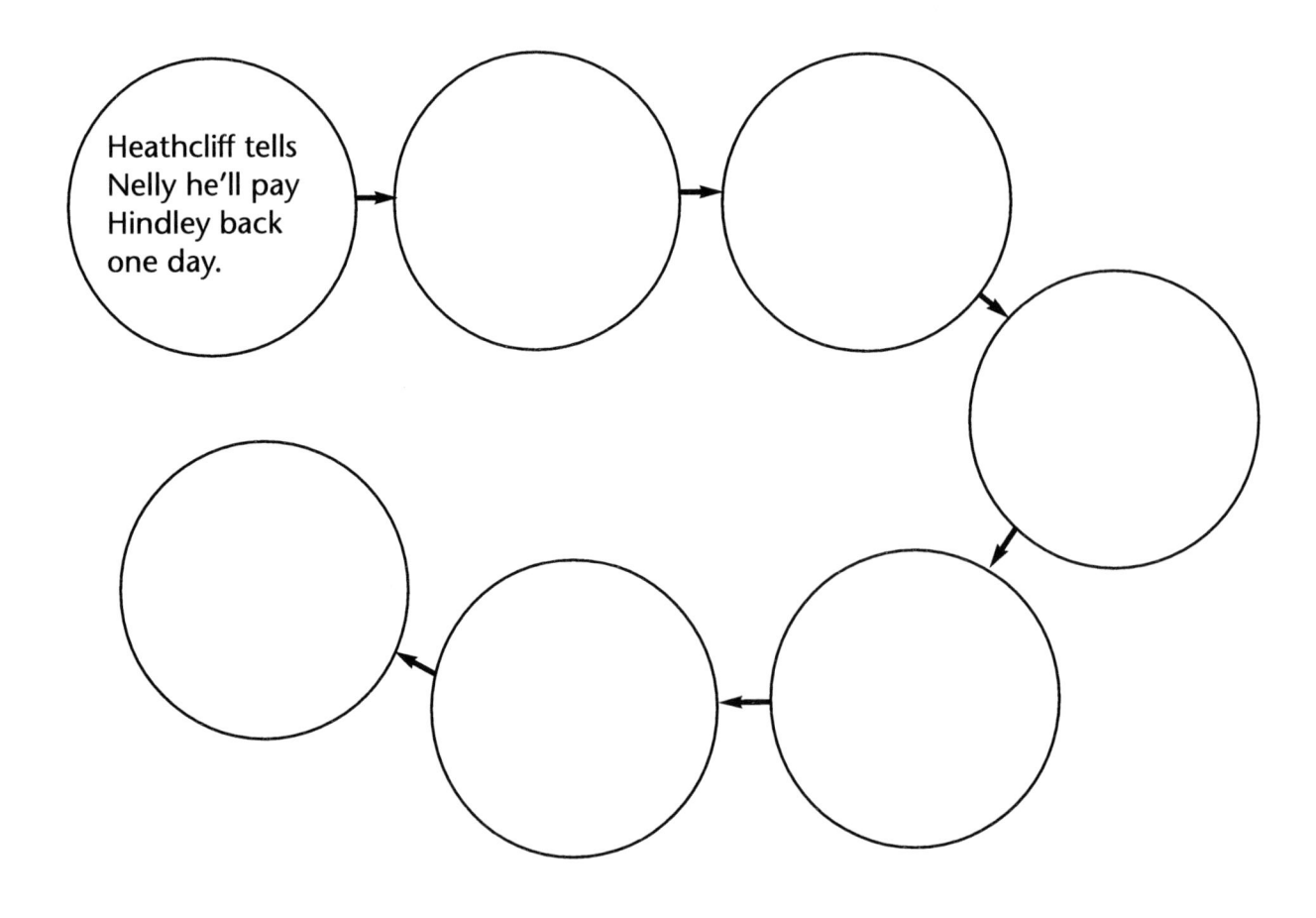

○ Heathcliff tells Nelly he'll pay Hindley back one day. → ○ → ○ → ○ → ○ → ○ → ○

© Novel Units, Inc.   18   All rights reserved

Name_____

Wuthering Heights
Activity #12: Character Comparison
Use After Reading

Directions: Place each character, by his or her letter, somewhere on each of the scales below. If you don't have enough information to make a definite decision, place the character's letter at "0."

A. Heathcliff   B. Edgar   C. Catherine Earnshaw   D. Hindley   E. Nelly

	3	2	1	0	1	2	3	
strong-willed								weak-willed
moody								even-tempered
dishonest								honest
intelligent								stupid
refined								ill-mannered
healthy								unhealthy
haughty								humble
nature-loving								indoor-loving
spiritual								down-to-earth

© Novel Units, Inc.   All rights reserved

Name_____

Wuthering Heights
Activity #13: Critical Thinking
Use After Reading

Directions: Some of the most powerful scenes in English Literature occur in *Wuthering Heights*. Rate each novel event listed according to the effect it had on you when you read it. It might help to picture these events as scenes in a movie version of the novel. Which would be the most and least dramatic? Rating scale: 3 = most powerful, 2 = moderately powerful, 1 = somewhat powerful, 0 = no emotional effect. Connect each mark with a colored pen when you are finished.

	Mr. Earnshaw brings Heathcliff home.	Heathcliff is sent home by the Lintons.	Mr. Lockwood dreams about Cathy.	Cathy collapses in Heathcliff's arms	Young Cathy & Nelly are held at the Heights.	Hindley drops Hareton over the railing.	Nelly finds Heathcliff, dead and sneering.
3							
2							
1							
0							

© Novel Units, Inc.

All rights reserved

Name_____

Wuthering Heights
Activity #14: Critical Analysis
Use During or After Reading

Directions: The poem below was written by Emily Brontë before she wrote *Wuthering Heights*. Read the poem and answer the questions to the right on the back of your paper.

Remembrance

Cold in the earth—and the deep snow piled above thee,
Far, far removed, cold in the dreary grave!
Have I forgot, my only Love, to love thee,
Severed at last by Time's all-severing wave?

Now, when alone, do my thoughts no longer hover
Over the mountains, on that northern shore,
Resting their wings where heath and fern leaves cover
Thy noble heart forever, ever more?

Cold in the earth—and fifteen wild Decembers,
From those brown hills, have melted into spring;
Faithful, indeed, is the spirit that remembers
After such years of change and suffering!

Sweet Love of youth, forgive, if I forget thee,
While the world's tide is bearing me along;
Other desires and other hopes beset me,
Hopes which obscure, but cannot do thee wrong!

No later light has lightened up my heaven,
No second morn has ever shown for me;
All my life's bliss from thy dear life was given,
All my life's bliss is in the grave with thee.

But, when the days of golden dreams had perished,
And even Despair was powerless to destroy,
Then did I learn how existence could be cherished,
Strengthened, and fed without the aid of joy.

Then did I check the tears of useless passion—
Weaned my young soul from yearning after thine;
Sternly denied its burning wish to hasten
Down to that tomb already more than mine.

And, even yet, I dare not let it languish,
Dare not indulge in memory's rapturous pain;
Once drinking deep of that divinest anguish,
How could I seek the empty world again?

1. Of the characters in *Wuthering Heights*, which one(s) might be the speaker(s)?

2. Who could be the subject of the poem?

3. What is "Time's all-severing wave"?

4. Does the speaker really ever forget the person who is in the grave?

5. What "burning wish" has the speaker managed to control?

6. What "divinest anguish" still tempts the speaker?

7. Summarize the meaning of the poem in one sentence.

© Novel Units, Inc.   All rights reserved

Name_____

Wuthering Heights
Activity #15: Creative Writing
Use After Reading

Directions: Young Cathy and Linton Heathcliff strike up a secret correspondence that continues until Nelly Dean finds the letters. The actual content of the letters is not revealed; we are simply told they are love letters. Below, write the first letter Cathy sent to Linton and his reply.

Thrushcross Grange
Summer, 1800

Dearest Linton,

Wuthering Heights
Summer, 1800

Dearest Cathy,

© Novel Units, Inc.

All rights reserved

Name_____

Wuthering Heights
Activity #16: Critical Thinking
Use After Reading

Directions: Some decisions made by characters in the novel are listed on the right. In the second column, list an alternate decision the character could have made. In the third column, write the probable results of the alternate decision.

Decision Made	Alternate Decision	Probable Results of Alternate Decision
Old Mr. Earnshaw decides to bring home a starving gypsy child.		
Catherine decides to marry Edgar Linton.		
Isabella decides to elope with Heathcliff.		
Young Cathy decides to become friends with Hareton and teach him to read.		

Name_____

Wuthering Heights
Activity #17: Review Activity
Use After Reading

Directions: Work in a small group or with a partner. Spend a few minutes on each square, brainstorming the topic listed. Jot down ideas that come to mind, and star items you need to study more closely.

Setting	Author	Main Characters
Style	Narrators	
Themes	Minor Characters	
	Conflicts	

Name_____

Wuthering Heights
Vocabulary Quiz

I. Matching: Write the letter of each word next to its correct definition.

_____ 1. imitated
_____ 2. large amount
_____ 3. generous
_____ 4. empty
_____ 5. wisdom
_____ 6. mentally imbalanced
_____ 7. heretical
_____ 8. one who is anti-social
_____ 9. without money or property
_____ 10. shouting
_____ 11. imperious
_____ 12. reprehensible
_____ 13. beginning to appear
_____ 14. apart
_____ 15. hard-hearted

| A. misanthropist |
| B. vapid |
| C. sagacity |
| D. vociferating |
| E. deranged |
| F. munificent |
| G. magisterial |
| H. heterodox |
| I. odious |
| J. incipient |
| K. copious |
| L. asunder |
| M. emulated |
| N. destitute |
| O. obdurate |

II. Sentence Completion: Choose the letter of the word that belongs in the blank.

_____ 16. The teachers without _____ lost their jobs.
   A. impertinence   B. avarice   C. trepidation   D. tenure

_____ 17. She was wearing a dress of soft _____.
   A. penetralium   B. curate   C. cambric   D. filial

_____ 18. When Jennifer forgot her lines in the play, she was _____.
   A. salubrious   B. churlish   C. languid   D. mortified

_____ 19. The fire _____ the plans for an addition to the house.
   A. obviated   B. usurped   C. dispatched   D. abjured

© Novel Units, Inc.

All rights reserved

Name_____

Wuthering Heights
Vocabulary Quiz • Page 2

_____ 20. The city council gave their _____ approval to the developers.
    A. dilatory   B. tacit   C. smiting   D. vigilant

_____ 21. He was overcome with a _____ of fear.
    A. interdict   B. paragon   C. bane   D. paroxysm

_____ 22. Her stepmother was the _____ of her existence.
    A. bane   B. elysium   C. epistle   D. execration

_____ 23. The _____ at the pep rally was deafening.
    A. immolation   B. avarice   C. appellation   D. clamour

_____ 24. "Please don't make me babysit again!" _____ Lauren.
    A. reproved   B. disenchanted C. importuned   D. deranged

_____ 25. Given two methods of getting the job done, Brad chose the most_____.
    A. expedient   B. diabolical   C. sundry   D. lachrymose

III. In each group of words below, three have something in common. Choose the word that does not belong.

_____ 26. A. misanthropist   B. blackguard   C. bane   D. sexton
_____ 27. A. soliloquised   B. dissented   C. discomfited   D. reproached
_____ 28. A. consumption   B. dissipation   C. iteration   D. malignancy
_____ 29. A. diabolical   B. vindictive   C. enigmatic   D. odious
_____ 30. A. compunction   B. epistle   C. disquietude   D. scruple

© Novel Units, Inc.   All rights reserved

Name_____

Wuthering Heights
Comprehension Quiz
Chapters I-XII

True-False: Indicate whether the statement is true or false. If it is false, rewrite it so that it is true.

_____ 1. The two estates in the novel are Wuthering Heights and Gateshead.

_____ 2. Hareton Earnshaw is Hindley's brother.

_____ 3. Catherine vows to haunt Heathcliff after she dies.

_____ 4. Isabella, Edgar, Heathcliff, and Catherine are all good friends.

_____ 5. Catherine and Edgar have been fairly happy since their marriage, in spite of Catherine's occasional depression.

_____ 6. Catherine decided to marry Edgar because she loves him more than she does Heathcliff.

_____ 7. In the three years he is gone, Heathcliff changes dramatically.

_____ 8. An example of Heathcliff's cruelty is that he kicks Isabella's favorite dog.

_____ 9. Catherine becomes delirious and refuses to eat after Edgar leaves.

_____ 10. The person who tells most of the story is Mr. Lockwood.

Quote Identification: After each quote, write the name of the person who said it.

11. "They may bury me twelve feet deep, and throw the church down over me, but I won't rest till you are with me. I never will!" _____

12. "Will you give up Heathcliff hereafter, or will you give up me?" _____

© Novel Units, Inc.   All rights reserved

Name_____

Wuthering Heights
Comprehension Quiz • Page 2

13. "I'm trying to settle how I shall pay Hindley back. I don't care how long I wait, if I can only do it at last." _____

14. "Proud people breed sad sorrows for themselves." _____

15. "He shall have his share of my hand if I catch him downstairs again till dark."

    _____

16. "Aw sud more likker look for th' horse; it 'ud be tuh more sense."

    _____

17. "You are a dog in the manger, Cathy, and desire no one to be loved but yourself!"

    _____

Short Answer.

18. How has Hareton changed since Heathcliff returned?

19. How has Hindley changed since the death of Frances?

20. What did Heathcliff and Isabella do, and what reasons did each have?

Name_____

Wuthering Heights
Comprehension Quiz
Chapters XIII-XXIV

Directions: *Wuthering Heights* is formed around a number of character-to-character relationships, some negative and some positive. At the left is a description of the interaction between two characters. Match each one with one of the character pairs listed on the right. (Note: Catherine Earnshaw is the older, Cathy Linton the younger.)

_____ 1. Although he is sickly and selfish, she loves him devotedly.

_____ 2. One vowed revenge on the other for being mistreated as a child.

_____ 3. She found it hard to believe he is her cousin.

_____ 4. Their love for the same woman ends in broken hearts all around.

_____ 5. She is now his sister in name only.

_____ 6. He calls her his life and his soul.

_____ 7. One saved the life of the other, then turned him into a brute.

_____ 8. She relates most of the story to him while he recuperates from an illness.

_____ 9. A devoted parent and a loving, if slightly willful, child.

_____ 10. She is used by him for financial gain and soon realizes her mistake.

_____ 11. One is a mother-figure to the other.

_____ 12. One is so contemptuous of the other that he calls him "it."

_____ 13. They are happily married for a while.

_____ 14. He calls her a witch.

A. Catherine Earnshaw and Heathcliff

B. Catherine Earnshaw and Edgar

C. Isabella and Edgar Linton

D. Isabella and Heathcliff

E. Cathy Linton and Linton Heathcliff

F. Nelly Dean and Cathy Linton

G. Heathcliff and Hindley

H. Heathcliff and Hareton

I. Edgar and Cathy Linton

J. Hareton and Cathy Linton

K. Heathcliff and Linton Heathcliff

L. Joseph and Cathy Linton

M. Mr. Lockwood and Nelly

N. Heathcliff and Edgar Linton

© Novel Units, Inc.　　　　29　　　　All rights reserved

Name_____

Wuthering Heights
Comprehension Quiz • Page 2

Multiple Choice: Choose the best answer for each item.

15. Nelly first learns about Isabella's misery through
    A. the newspaper.   B. Zillah.   C. Joseph.   D. a letter.

16. Heathcliff demands that Nelly arrange a meeting between himself and
    A. Hindley.   B. Edgar.   C. Catherine.   D. Fanny.

17. At their last meeting, Heathcliff and Catherine
    A. quarrel bitterly.
    B. vow to be together in the afterlife.
    C. forgive one another.
    D. all of these

18. Catherine is buried
    A. with the Lintons.
    B. in a corner of the churchyard.
    C. with the Earnshaws.
    D. none of these

19. When Isabella escaped from Wuthering Heights, she went first to
    A. Thrushcross Grange .
    B. Penistone Crags.
    C. London.
    D. Gimmerton.

20. Linton Heathcliff finds little favor with his father because he
    A. is spiritless and self-pitying like his mother.
    B. has tuberculosis.
    C. constantly quotes the Bible.
    D. doesn't get along with Hareton.

Name_____

Wuthering Heights
Unit Exam • Level I

Multiple Choice: Choose the best answer for each item. (Note: Throughout this exam, "Catherine Earnshaw" is used to refer to the elder Catherine and "Cathy Linton" is used to refer to her daughter.)

1. The one character who is the catalyst for most of the action and emotion in the novel is
   A. Nelly Dean.
   B. Heathcliff.
   C. Lockwood.
   D. Catherine Earnshaw.

2. All of the following details about Linton Heathcliff show him to be rather weak except
   A. his reaction to Cathy's push.
   B. his behavior on the day he arrived.
   C. his physical appearance.
   D. his intellect.

3. *Wuthering Heights* is told from a(n)_____ point of view by _____.
   A. omniscient; Nellie and Lockwood
   B. third-person; Emily Brontë
   C. first person; Nellie and Lockwood
   D. third person omniscient; Emily Brontë

4. The structure of Brontë's novel is unique in that
   A. she begins in the present, then flashes back in time, then continues in the present tense.
   B. she has divided it into an unusually large number of chapters.
   C. it is rather long and slow in pace.
   D. she uses a lot of imagery.

5. The primary conflict in the novel is between
   A. old and young.
   B. literacy and illiteracy.
   C. good and evil.
   D. Wuthering Heights and Thrushcross Grange.

© Novel Units, Inc.   All rights reserved

Name_____

Wuthering Heights
Unit Exam • Level I • page 2

6. Emily Brontë's choice of names to create a desired effect is evident in the case of
   A. Throttler, Gnasher and Wolf—Heathcliff's dogs.
   B. Skulker, the watchdog.
   C. Fanny, Isabella's lapdog.
   D. all of the above.

7. Heathcliff's feelings toward his son could be best described as
   A. fondness and pride.   C. indifference and apathy.
   B. contempt and disgust.   D. resentment and anger.

8. Catherine Earnshaw was
   A. gentle and cooperative.   C. spirited and willful.
   B. usually able to get her way. D. both B and C

9. Catherine and Hareton's plan to replace a plot of blackcurrant trees with flowers represents
   A. a new beginning for their lives.   C. another failure.
   B. a shared interest in horticulture. D. a rebirth of evil intentions.

10. Although Joseph is a faithful church-goer and Bible-quoter, ironically he also
    A. is an atheist.   C. is a traitor to the Earnshaws.
    B. gossips, criticizes, and makes trouble.   D. speaks in a Yorkshire dialect.

11. Cathy's and Linton's contrasting ideas of "the pleasantest manner of spending a hot July day" show
    A. the use of symbolism for character development.
    B. that opposites attract.
    C. the many moods of Yorkshire weather.
    D. how Linton liked activity while Cathy preferred drowsy calm.

Name_____

Wuthering Heights
Unit Exam • Level I • page 3

12. Heathcliff sought revenge through all of the following methods except
    A. marrying Isabella.
    B. visiting Catherine at the Grange.
    C. gambling with Hindley.
    D. degrading Hareton.

13. In addition to loving Catherine, Heathcliff also cared about
    A. old Joseph.
    B. Hareton.
    C. Nelly Dean.
    D. Isabella.

14. Isabella's letter to Nelly revealed she was
    A. a contented new wife.
    B. still angry with Edgar.
    C. desperately unhappy.
    D. still in love with Heathcliff.

15. Despite Catherine's illness, she _____ before she died.
    A. walked out on the moor to meet Heathcliff
    B. chased Edgar with a knife
    C. wrote a letter to Hindley
    D. gave birth to a child

16. As Edgar Linton approached death, he worried
    A. that he would not be buried near Catherine.
    B. about Cathy falling into the hands of Heathcliff.
    C. because Cathy was not the heir to Thrushcross Grange.
    D. that Linton would squander all the family's assets.

17. Heathcliff was able to lure Nelly and Cathy into Wuthering Heights and hold them captive for five days because
    A. Edgar had died and could not come to their aid.
    B. Hareton used force on the two women.
    C. when Cathy's pony became lame, she sought help at the Heights.
    D. Linton implored them to come because Heathcliff said Linton could not re-enter the house without Cathy.

18. Heathcliff revealed that he bribed the sexton to
   A. have Edgar buried in a different plot than the one in which Catherine is buried.
   B. move Catherine's coffin to a different location.
   C. sell him a space next to Catherine.
   D. strike one side of Catherine's coffin loose and do the same to his when he is buried beside her so that their ashes will mingle.

19. When Cathy made friends with _____, things began to look up for her.
   A. Joseph
   B. Heathcliff
   C. Zillah
   D. Hareton

20. Heathcliff's body was found by
   A. Zillah
   B. Hareton
   C. Joseph
   D. Nelly Dean

Quote Identification: In each group, choose the character on the right that matches the quote on the left.

_____ 21. "Why have I made him angry by taking your part, then, a hundred times?"

_____ 22. "Disturbed her? No! She has disturbed me, night and day, through eighteen years—incessantly—remorselessly—"

_____ 23. "Catherine, Catherine, I'm a traitor too, and I dare not tell you! But leave me and I shall be killed!"

_____ 24. "Damn the hellish villain! He knocks at the door as if he were master here already!"

A. Cathy Linton
B. Heathcliff
C. Hareton
D. Linton
E. Hindley
F. Nelly Dean
G. Catherine Earnshaw
H. Joseph
I. Isabella

Name_____

Wuthering Heights
Unit Exam • Level I • page 5

_____ 25. "You'd better seek shelter somewhere else tonight! Mr. Earnshaw has a mind to shoot you if you persist in endeavouring to enter!"

_____ 26. "I wish I could hold you till we were both dead!"

_____ 27. "If he loved with all the powers of his puny being, he couldn't love as much in eighty years as I could in a day!"

A. Cathy Linton
B. Heathcliff
C. Hareton
D. Linton
E. Hindley
F. Nelly Dean
G. Catherine Earnshaw
H. Joseph
I. Isabella

_____ 28. "Poor lad! —he's witched, Aw'm sartin on 't! O Lord, judge 'em, fur they's norther law nur justice amang wer rullers!"

_____ 29. "I know why Hareton never speaks when I am in the kitchen. He is afraid I shall laugh at him."

_____ 30. "I shall envy no one on their wedding day: there won't be a happier woman than myself in England!"

True-False:

_____ 31. Heathcliff was interested in Isabella only because she was Edgar's heir.

_____ 32. Brontë sometimes used the weather to indicate the mood of the novel.

_____ 33. Hindley could not attend Catherine's funeral because he was already near death himself.

_____ 34. Heathcliff had nothing to do with Linton's letters to Edgar.

_____ 35. Linton was not afraid of his father and often spoke rudely to him.

_____ 36. Linton helped Cathy escape from Wuthering Heights.

_____ 37. Nelly Dean was engaged to be married at the end of the novel.

_____ 38. Heathcliff kept the half of Cathy's locket that held her mother's picture.

© Novel Units, Inc.

All rights reserved

Name_____

Wuthering Heights
Unit Exam • Level I • page 6

_____ 39. Both Hareton and Cathy remind Heathcliff of Hindley.

_____ 40. Lockwood tried to get his rent money back from Heathcliff since he was not going to be there for half the term of the lease.

Matching: Match the character on the right with the action on the left.

_____ 41. Brought home a starving gypsy child.

_____ 42. Was a playmate and later a servant at Wuthering Heights and at Thrushcross.

_____ 43. Was patient with his wife's gloomy moods until he saw her obvious delight at the return of his old enemy.

_____ 44. Nearly lost his life when his father dropped him from a second-floor railing.

A. Catherine Earnshaw
B. Old Mr. Earnshaw
C. Hindley
D. Nelly Dean
E. Isabella
F. Edgar
G. Heathcliff
H. Hareton
I. Cathy Linton
J. Linton

_____ 45. His illness, weakness, and self-pity all came from a lack of self-esteem.

_____ 46. Died of fever, starvation, and possibly of a broken heart.

_____ 47. Hated being displaced in his father's affections by an orphan, and did all he could to pay back the interloper.

_____ 48. Her infatuation with Heathcliff brought her nothing but misery.

_____ 49. His primary purpose in life was to get revenge.

_____ 50. Had her mother's willfulness and dark eyes, her father's more gentle temperament and fair hair.

Name_____

Wuthering Heights
Unit Exam • Level II

I. **Critical Thinking:** Choose two of the topics below. Write a well-developed essay for each. Be sure to include specific examples and details from the novel. Indicate the topics on which you decide to write.

   A. The structure of *Wuthering Heights* is very different from other novels written during this period. Explain the differences, and how the author managed to tell the story using several different narrators.

   B. Choose an answer to the following question, and write an essay defending your choice: The primary theme of *Wuthering Heights* is
   (a) social imprisonment versus spiritual freedom
   (b) good versus evil
   (c) impermanence of self; permanence of something larger
   (d) revenge destroys the avenger

   C. Choose a pair of characters from the list below. Write a comparison/contrast essay about them.
   (a) Catherine Earnshaw and Heathcliff
   (b) Edgar Linton and Heathcliff
   (c) Isabella Linton and Catherine Earnshaw
   (d) Catherine Earnshaw and her daughter

II. **Creative Writing:** Choose one of the topics below.

   D. Write a poem about one of the characters in the novel.

   E. Write an obituary notice for Heathcliff.

   F. Write a letter of condolence to Hareton about Heathcliff's death.

   G. Write a story about a walk you take one rainy evening out on the moor near the churchyard.

   H. Write a letter of congratulations to Hareton and Cathy after their wedding.

Answer Key

Note: Since many of the activities are designed to promote critical and creative thinking, individual responses will vary and no answers are given for those marked "Answers will vary."

Activity #1: Answers will vary.

Activity #2: Answers will vary. Check for participation by all group members.

Activity #3: 1. equanimity; 2. dissipation; 3. blackguard; 4. compunction; 5. scruple; 6. paroxysm; 7. avarice; 8. deranged; 9. dilatory; 10. sovereign; 11. prognosticate; 12. propitiate; 13. protract; 14. munificent; 15. consumption

Activity #4:

Across: 2. COMMINATIONS; 6. DIABOLICAL; 7. SCINTILLATING; 9. QUIESCENCE; 12. APPELLATION; 13. HETERODOX; 15. SLATTERN; 16. ABJECT; 18. INSIPID; 19. WICKET; 20. THIBLE; 21. DREE; 22. AUDACITY

Down: 1. ITERATE; 3. DISQUIETUDE; 4. OAVATT (AVARICIOUS); 5. ARTICULATION; 8. DESPONDENCY; 10. IMPORTUNE; 11. MISGIVINGS; 14. SANGUINE; 17. ODIOUS

© Novel Units, Inc. All rights reserved

Activity #5: Answers will vary. Sample: **Mortified,** *she wept* **copious** tears as she watched the **immolation** of the **epistles** from her secret lover.

Activity #6: Answers will vary. Sample, #1: "…the hollowness around them transforming to gaunt madness the peaceful expression they once wore."

Activity #7: 1. destitute; 2. adroitly; 3. fortnight; 4. bane; 5. vigilance; 6. smiting; 7. retaliate; 8. condescend; 9. monomania; 10. obdurate; 11. paragon; 12. reproved; 13. disenchanted

Activity #8: Answers will vary, however Thrushcross Grange is stately and conventional, inhabited by refined people who behave properly. It is in the valley, protected from the weather. Wuthering Heights is run down and inhabited by strange folk with strange activities; up in the hills, it is exposed to the "wuthering" winds. Both are English homes for the privileged class; both have servants, stables, and farm laborers. Both are in remote settings, close to the moor.

Activity #9: Mr. Linton and Mrs. Linton both died in 1780; Mr. Earnshaw died in 1777, Mrs. Earnshaw in 1773. Heathcliff's date of birth is uncertain (approximately 1764); he died in 1802. Isabella was born in 1765 and died in 1797. Edgar was born in 1762, died in 1801. Catherine Earnshaw was born in 1765, died in 1784. Hindley was born in 1757, died in 1784. Frances, whose birth date is unknown, died in 1778. Linton, born in 1784, died in 1801. Catherine Linton was born in 1784, and Hareton in 1778.

Activity #10: Students' answers will vary somewhat but should give a good representation of the feelings between the various characters and Heathcliff. He uses Isabella, Linton, Young Cathy, and Hareton in his revenge scheme against Hindley and Edgar, whom he despises. Nelly is also a tool in his game, although he does confide in her and tolerate her. Catherine, of course, he loves obsessively and the feeling is mutual. Of the other characters mentioned, only Hareton seems to care at all about Heathcliff. The rest hate him—although Nelly does have some pity for him.

Activity #11: Students may not have the same events listed, but they should list those that led to the realization of Heathcliff's revenge plans.

Activity #12: Answers will vary and should be discussed.

Activity #13: Answers will vary.

Activity #14: 1. Heathcliff or Edgar after Catherine's death, or Hindley after Frances' death. 2. Catherine or Frances 3. death 4. no 5. the wish to be dead also 6. being dead and with the loved one 7. Although the loved one has been dead fifteen years, the speaker has not forgotten and still often wishes for the release from mourning that death would bring.

Activity #15: Answers will vary.

Activity #16: Answers will vary.

Activity #17: Answers will vary. Check to be sure charts are being completed.

Study Guide Answers

Chapters I-VI

1. ominous, dark, confusing; the wind, horses in the stables, Joseph yelling, dogs barking
2. He appears to be a gentleman but Lockwood feels he may not be. No.
3. Mrs. Heathcliff and Hareton. No.
4. the phrase regarding the "odd notion" Heathcliff had about the bedchamber
5. He reads the diaries and notes of Catherine Earnshaw. Later a Cathy Linton appears in his dream, clawing at the window to be let in from the cold.
6. He calls for Cathy to come in.
7. Nelly Dean, Lockwood's housekeeper, takes over as narrator.
8. A foundling, Heathcliff was a favorite of old Mr. Earnshaw, and this did not set well with Hindley, the real son.
9. She is rather wild and willful, very emotional, but also quite lovable.
10. He detests him.
11. He detests Hindley.
12. Hindley returns to take charge of things, and is very cruel in his treatment of Heathcliff.
13. They consider Cathy a victim of both Heathcliff's evil influence and her brother's neglect. They keep Cathy at Thrushcross but send Heathcliff away as if he is some kind of villain.

Chapters VII-XII

14. She returns a refined young lady.
15. She makes fun of his slovenly appearance. He is hurt.
16. She explains that she is very well-read.
17. He turns to drinking and gambling and acts half crazy; he takes no joy in fatherhood.
18. Heathcliff. He realizes if he had let Hareton die, Hindley would have been ruined by the guilt he would bear and Heathcliff's plan for revenge would have been realized with little effort.
19. whether to marry Edgar Linton
20. Catherine imagines she would then have the means to help Heathcliff complete his education and become a gentleman.
21. no
22. Her love for Edgar is changeable like foliage; her love for Heathcliff is like the rocks.
23. While Catherine waits futilely for him to return, she catches a chill. While recuperating at the Grange, she infects Mr. and Mrs. Linton, who die.
24. Edgar sees Catherine's extreme affection for him and is jealous.
25. Heathcliff has taught Hareton to swear and to call Hindley "devil Daddy."

© Novel Units, Inc.   All rights reserved

26. He is trying to get Hindley's fortune through gambling.
27. Nelly finds her hung by a handkerchief, saving her just in time.
28. She has decided she's angry at both of them, and that she will break their hearts by breaking her own. She becomes ill.

Chapters XIII-XVIII
29. She is ignored, berated.
30. The information Nelly relates came to her in the form of a letter from Isabella, which is quoted in full.
31. Edgar couldn't love her as much in 80 years as he can in one day.
32. Her property became his upon their marriage, and she is the heir to Thrushcross.
33. She claims she will haunt Heathcliff until he joins her in death.
34. Answers will vary.
35. to replace Isabella as the heir to Thrushcross
36. He is devastated, crashes his head against a tree and howls like a beast.
37. The change back to cold and damp weather seems to parallel the grief felt for the loss of Catherine.
38. Crazy, alcoholic, and now no longer in possession of his property, Hindley dies.
39. Heathcliff is planning to make Hareton as crude as he himself is.
40. Isabella escapes, stops at Thrushcross, and talks with Nelly.
41. to London, where she has a son and then dies 12 years later
42. She has her mother's personality to some extent, but it is softened by her father's mild temper. Her eyes are like her mother's, but her hair is fair like her father's.
43. She rides her pony off Grange property and arrives at the Heights, where Hareton takes her on a tour. She finds it hard to believe he's her cousin.

Chapters XIX-XXIV
44. He looks like Edgar, pale and weak, and is something like Edgar was when he was younger, i.e. spoiled and whiny. But even Edgar wasn't as bad as Linton, and Edgar has shown himself to be a decent person since his youth.
45. Through Linton, Heathcliff will control Thrushcross Grange.
46. four years
47. Heathcliff has degraded Hareton and made him into a brute. In spite of this, they have a fondness for one another.
48. Cathy and Linton are secretly sending love letters.
49. She is lovesick and depressed.
50. Linton, according to Heathcliff, is beside himself with sorrow and is likely to die of a broken heart.
51. Answers will vary. Cathy is very tolerant of Linton, in spite of his peevish manner.
52. While Nelly and her father are ill, Cathy rides her pony over to the Heights.

53. He explains how unworthy he feels. His lack of self-esteem makes it impossible for him to be loving toward anyone else.
54. Edgar agrees to allow Linton to come to the Grange, but Heathcliff will not allow this, so it is agreed the two young people can meet on the moor between the two places, with Nelly as chaperone.

Chapters XXV-XXIX
55. He is very ill and knows he is dying.
56. that he is in good health and a much more responsible and caring person than he really is
57. Edgar realizes it is the only way for Cathy to remain at Thrushcross.
58. Heathcliff is engineering the meeting between the two. It's important that Linton appear to be strong so that Edgar won't object to Cathy marrying him.
59. He lures Nelly and Cathy to Wuthering Heights, where they are trapped by Heathcliff.
60. marry Linton
61. She does not know if her father is alive or dead.
62. He is the one who helps Cathy escape in time to say goodbye to her dying father.
63. Linton is not old enough to have title to property, so his father controls it.
64. Uncover Catherine's coffin and take off one side of it.
65. Take off the facing side of his coffin and bury him next to Catherine so their dust can mingle.

Chapters XXX-XXXIV
66. He signed everything, including all of Cathy's possessions, over to Heathcliff.
67. She is bitter and very sad. She has lost her father, Nelly is no longer with her, she is destitute, and she is forced to work like a servant for a man she detests.
68. He can't read, and his attempts are amusing to her.
69. eight months
70. There is a splendid moon, the gates and doors at Wuthering Heights are open; there is a friendlier mood about the place now.
71. He became more cruel and heartless than ever, resorting to physical violence against Cathy, who refuses to bend completely to his will. Hareton, however, has learned to read and is trying to look more presentable.
72. He seemed to know he was going to die soon, and felt that Catherine was waiting for him.
73. Heathcliff became obsessed with joining Catherine in death, and decided to quit eating and let himself die, just as Catherine did.
74. Answers will vary. One might say that Heathcliff's hatred destroyed many people, himself included. On the other hand, the love between Cathy and Hareton seems to absolve past enmity. Even Heathcliff is content to let them be and has no more desire for revenge.

Vocabulary Quiz

1.	M	11.	G	21.	D
2.	K	12.	I	22.	A
3.	F	13.	J	23.	D
4.	B	14.	L	24.	C
5.	C	15.	O	25.	A
6.	E	16.	D	26.	D
7.	H	17.	C	27.	C
8.	A	18.	D	28.	C
9.	N	19.	A	29.	C
10.	D	20.	B	30.	B

Comprehension Quiz, Chapters I-XII

1. F
2. F
3. T
4. F
5. T
6. F
7. T
8. F
9. F
10. F
11. Catherine Earnshaw
12. Edgar
13. Heathcliff
14. Nelly Dean
15. Hindley
16. Joseph
17. Isabella
18. Heathcliff has taught him to swear and behave crudely.
19. He has become a drunk and a gambler.
20. They eloped, Isabella due to infatuation and Heathcliff because she is Edgar's heir.

Comprehension Quiz, Chapters XIII-XXIV

1.	E	11.	F
2.	G	12.	K
3.	J	13.	B
4.	N	14.	L
5.	C	15.	D
6.	A	16.	C
7.	H	17.	D
8.	M	18.	B
9.	I	19.	A
10.	D	20.	A

© Novel Units, Inc.   All rights reserved

Unit Exam, Level I

1.	B	11.	A	21.	C	31.	T	41.	B
2.	D	12.	B	22.	B	32.	T	42.	D
3.	C	13.	B	23.	D	33.	F	43.	F
4.	A	14.	C	24.	E	34.	F	44.	H
5.	C	15.	D	25.	I	35.	F	45.	J
6.	D	16.	C	26.	G	36.	T	46.	A
7.	B	17.	D	27.	B	37.	F	47.	C
8.	D	18.	D	28.	H	38.	T	48.	E
9.	A	19.	D	29.	A	39.	F	49.	G
10.	B	20.	D	30.	F	40.	F	50.	I

Unit Exam, Level II

I. A. Should include: present-past-present structure, different narrators and methods, and the novel's "shocking" themes (for their time).
    B. Any answer may be chosen; all are defensible.
    C. Answers will vary with choice of characters.

II. One creative topic should be chosen.

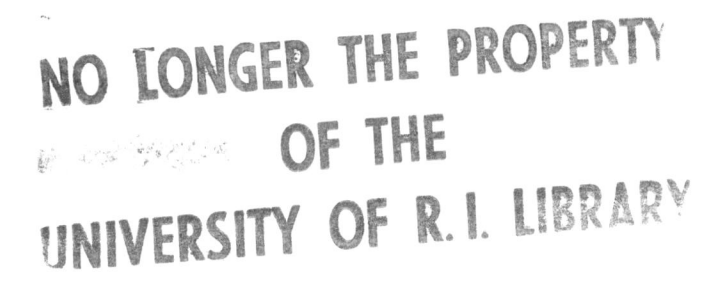

© Novel Units, Inc.   All rights reserved

AIM HIGHER

English Study Guide and Workbook

SHEPHERD • CASTRO • SKEA • CHOI

LEVEL B

aim
advanced instructional materials

The Future of Education, Today

Beverly, Massachusetts
Farmingdale, New Jersey

aim higher!

STAFF CREDITS:

PUBLISHER
  Robert D. Shepherd

EDITORIAL STAFF
  Diane Perkins Castro
  Annie Sun Choi
  Kelsey Stevenson Skea

PRODUCTION & DESIGN STAFF
  Matthew Pasquerella

OTHER CONTRIBUTOR
  Michelle Castro

No part of this publication may be stored in an information retrieval system or reproduced in any form—by photocopying, scanning, reproduction in a database, posting on the Internet, or by any other means—without prior written permission from the publisher.

© 2001 Advanced Instructional Materials, Inc.
All rights reserved.

First Edition

Printed in the United States of America

05 04 03 02 01   10 9 8 7 6 5 4 3 2 1

ISBN: 1-58171-265-0

Advanced Instructional Materials, Inc.
100 Cummings Center, Suite 146Q
Beverly, MA 01915
Sales Office: 1–800–552–1377
Visit our Web site at http://www.higheraim.com

Table of Contents

INTRODUCTION   Glossary for Introduction   1

SELECTION 1   Glossary for *A Chair for My Mother*   1

                     Word Search   3

                     Writing Practice   4

LESSONS 1–6   Glossary for Lessons   5

                     Finish the Sentence   6

                     Writing Practice   7

SELECTION 2   Glossary for "All About Koalas"   8

                     Word Clues   9

                     Writing Practice   10

SELECTION 3   Glossary for "The Apple Tree"   11

                     Word Mix-Up   12

                     Writing Practice   13

SELECTION 4   Glossary for "Give It a Spin"   14

                     Secret Code   15

                     Writing Practice   16

SELECTION 5	Glossary for "Chasing"	17
	Match the Picture	17
	Writing Practice	18
SELECTION 6	Glossary for "The Ugly Duckling"	19
	Fill in the Blank	20
	Writing Practice	21
SELECTION 7	Glossary for "Around the World in Twenty Days"	22
	Word Whiz	23
	Writing Practice	24
SELECTION 8	Glossary for "A Park Named Yellowstone"	25
	Crossword Puzzle	26
	Writing Practice	27
SELECTION 9	Glossary for "Up in the Sky"	28
	Word Search	28
	Writing Practice	29
SELECTION 10	Glossary for "White House Pets"	30
	Whose Pet Is It?	31
	Writing Practice	32

Level B Glossary and Workbook

Introduction	
PAGE IV	
pretend journeys	make-believe trips
practice	do something over and over again to get better at it

from *A Chair for My Mother*	
PAGE 1	
apartment	part of a building where people live
neighbors	people who live near you
rug	floor covering
pots and pans	metal dishes for cooking
silverware	spoons, forks, and knives
cousin	child of your uncle or aunt
stuffed bear	soft toy that looks like a bear
PAGE 2	
clapped	made noise by hitting hands together
speech	something you say in front of many people
kindest	nicest
sofa	couch; big, soft chair
load	something you carry
hum	sing a song quietly without the words
comfortable	relaxed
diner	small restaurant
wrappers	papers to cover something
day off	day when you do not go to school or work
downtown	middle of the city, where stores are

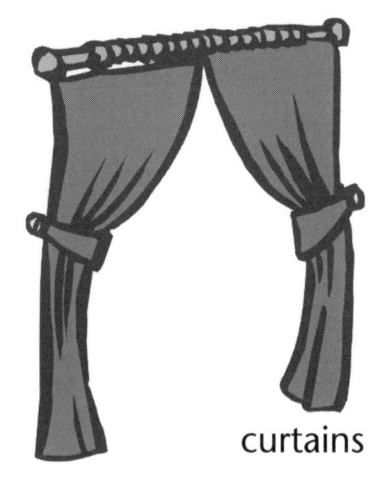

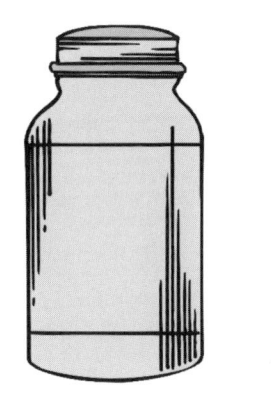

curtains

jar

coins

Level B Glossary and Workbook: English 1

PAGE 3	
saving	keeping for later
PAGE 4	
contest	game in which one person wins something
PAGE 5	
trade	give something and get something back in return
mean	not nice

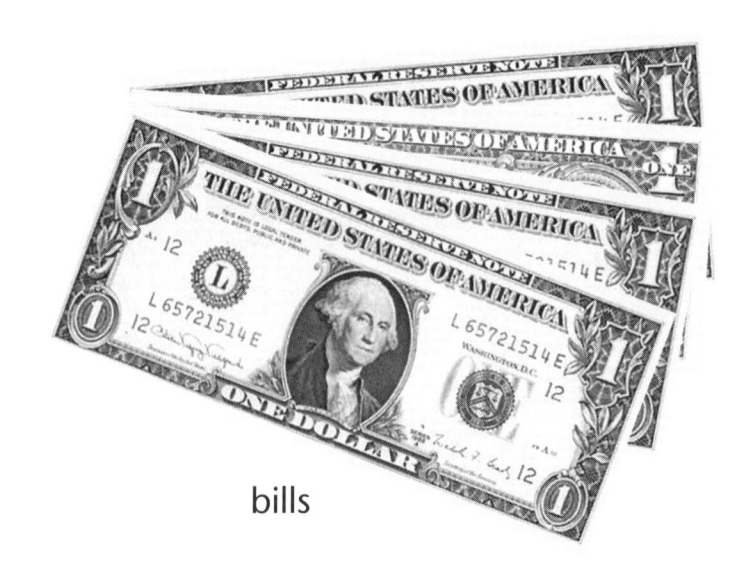

tacos

pancakes

bills

Word Search

Directions: Look for these words from *A Chair for My Mother*. The words may go from up to down or left to right in the puzzle. When you find a word in the puzzle, circle it. One word has been circled for you.

    apartment   jar
    coins   pans
√cousin   rug
    curtains   sofa
    hum   tacos

C	O	U	S	I	N	J	X	Z
U	A	E	P	P	T	S	C	S
R	U	G	W	I	V	U	O	M
T	B	G	R	B	C	Q	I	F
A	P	A	R	T	M	E	N	T
I	A	F	P	N	H	T	S	A
N	N	X	W	T	S	F	F	C
S	S	O	F	A	W	P	Q	O
J	C	B	B	L	G	L	I	S
A	L	F	W	T	N	W	Z	D
R	D	C	H	B	Y	H	U	M

Level B Glossary and Workbook: English   3

✍ Writing Practice

Writing Prompt: If you saved lots of money what would you buy? Write a few sentences about it on the lines below.

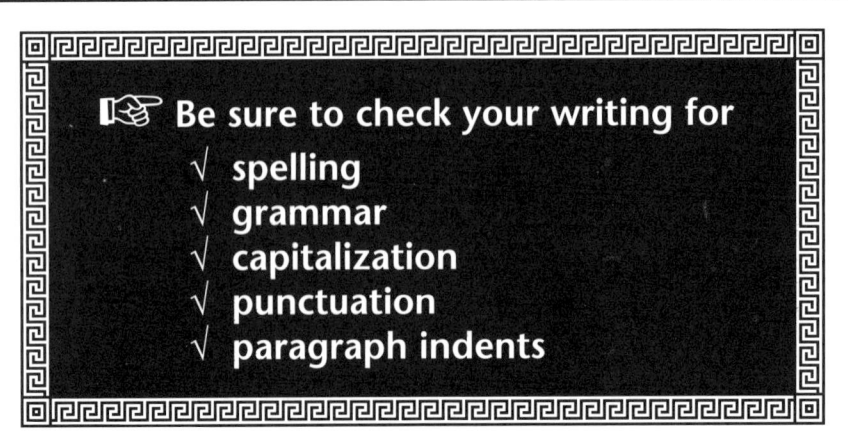

☞ **Be sure to check your writing for**
- √ spelling
- √ grammar
- √ capitalization
- √ punctuation
- √ paragraph indents

Lessons

PAGE 6
whole	everything together
therefore	so

PAGE 7
tips	hints to help you do better
rule out	cross out; get rid of

PAGE 8
information	facts about something
carefully	slowly, with care

PAGE 9
ruler	flat stick used to measure how long things are

PAGE 10
event	something that happens
finally	at the end
dates	when something happens

PAGE 11
cause	what makes something happen
bleed	to let out blood
petting	patting an animal's fur
purr	sound a cat makes when it is happy
"how come"	why

PAGE 12
figure out	find out the answer; discover
make sense	sound right

gift

keys

Level B Glossary and Workbook: English

Finish the Sentence

Directions: Choose the right word from the Word Bank to fill in each blank. Each word can be used only once.

Word Bank

bleeding	make sense
gifts	petting
information	tip
jar	whole

1. The little girl put coins in the _____.

2. It is Ana's birthday. Her friends will give her _____.

3. Ming fell down and cut his knee. His knee is _____.

4. Chris didn't understand the question. It did not _____ _____ to him.

5. At the _____ zoo you can touch and feed the animals.

6. Remember to read the _____ story, not just part of it.

7. Ms. Tyler gave us a _____ about writing. She said we should write about what we know.

8. Where can I find _____ about zebras?.

✍ Writing Practice

Writing Prompt: Tell the three most helpful ideas you learned in the Lessons. Write one good sentence for each idea.

1. _____

_____

2. _____

_____

3. _____

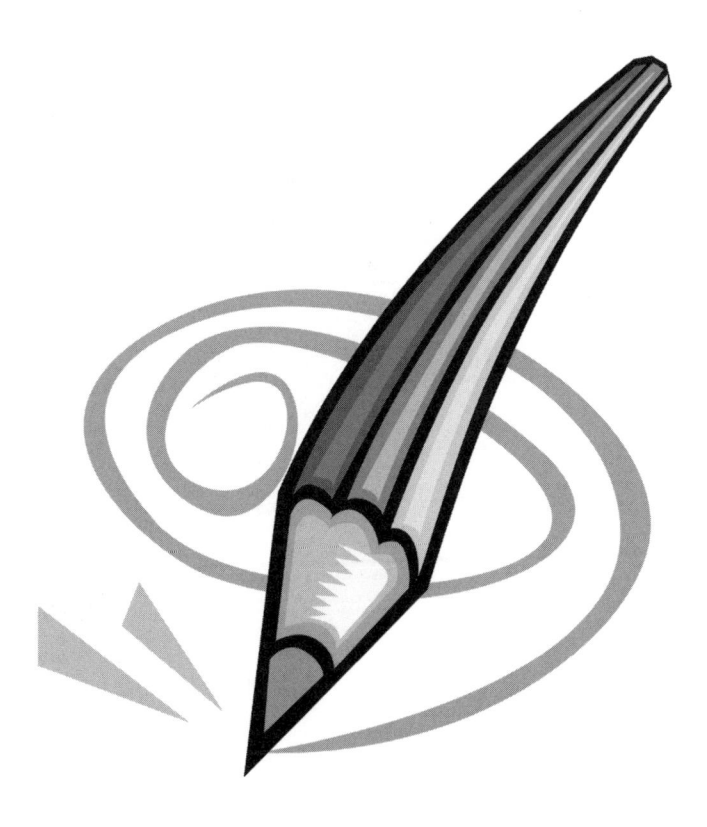

Level B Glossary and Workbook: English   7

"All About Koalas"

PAGE 16	
fur	hair on an animal
leaves	green parts of a tree
eucalyptus	kind of tree that grows in Australia
store	keep
PAGE 17	
chopped	cut
PAGE 18	
Antarctica	large, cold place where the South Pole is
zoo	place where people can see many animals
PAGE 19	
peel	take the skin off
swim	move in the water
PAGE 20	
lonely	feeling alone and sad

kangaroo

opossum

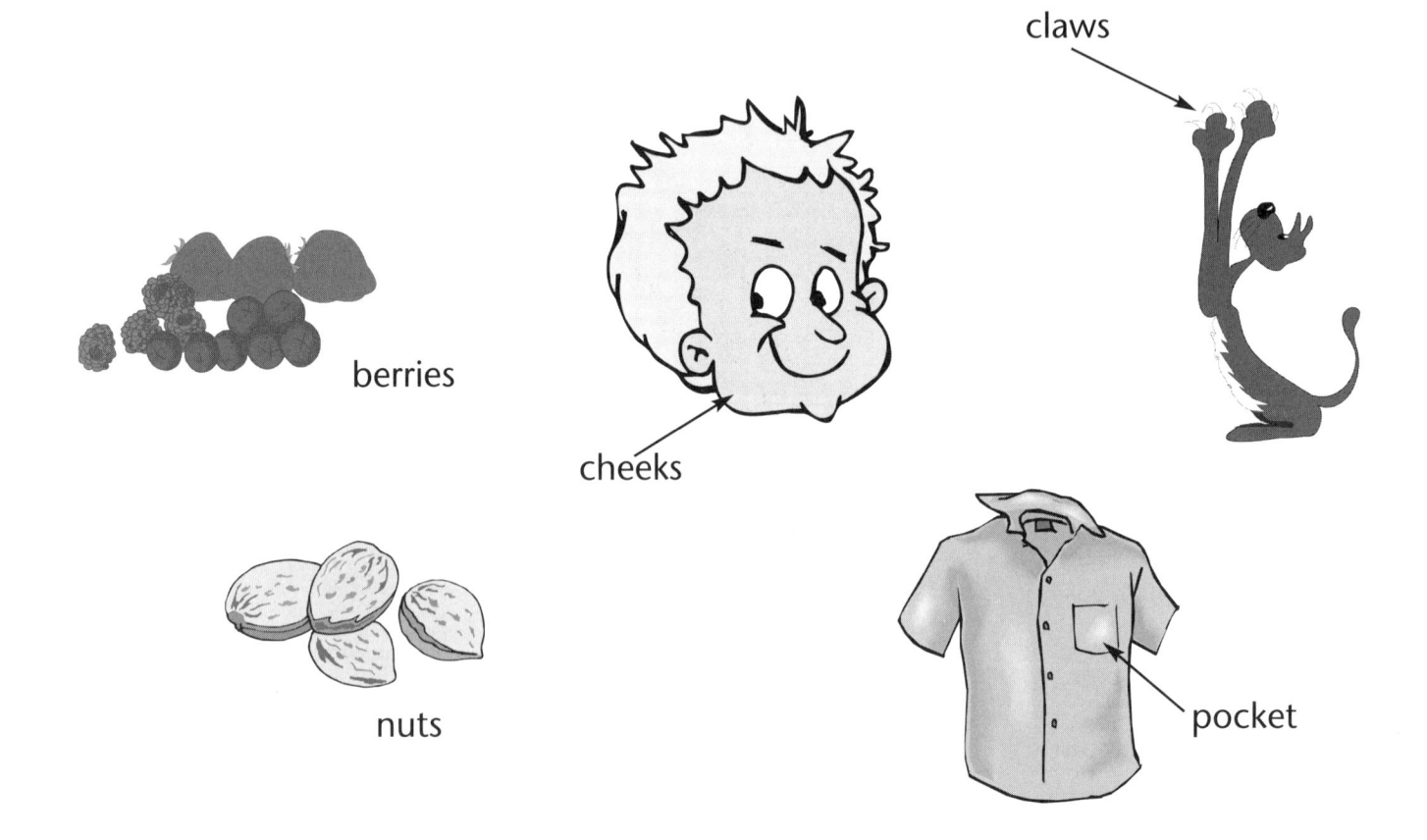

berries

cheeks

claws

nuts

pocket

8   AIM Higher! Reading Comprehension: Level B

Word Clues

Directions: Draw a line from the word to the clue that matches it. The first one is done for you.

1. leaves   a. keeps animals warm

2. pocket   b. a kind of tree

3. claws   c. how you feel when you have no one to play with

4. fur   d. place where some animals live

5. swim   e. parts of a tree

6. cheeks   f. a place to put money in your pants

7. koala   g. sharp and strong fingernails

8. zoo   h. part of your face

9. eucalyptus   i. move in the water

10. lonely   j. an animal that lives in Australia

Level B Glossary and Workbook: English   9

✍ Writing Practice

Writing Prompt: Why are there fewer koalas than there used to be? Write your answer to the question on the lines below.

☞ Be sure to check your writing for
- √ spelling
- √ grammar
- √ capitalization
- √ punctuation
- √ paragraph indents

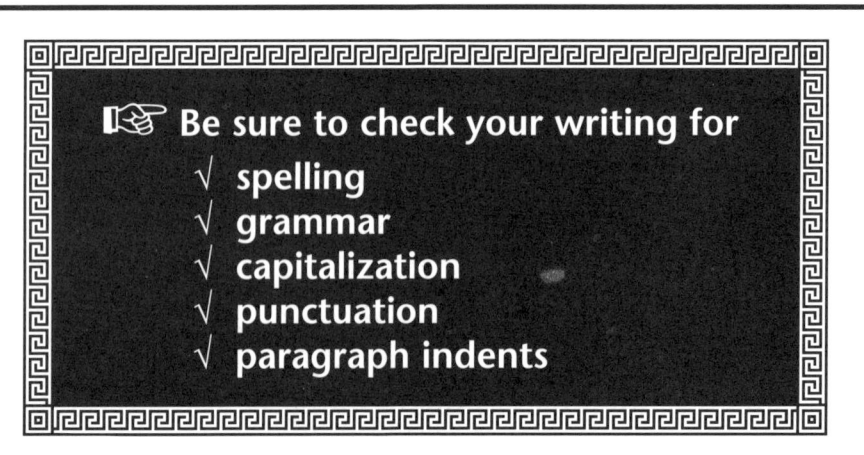

"The Apple Tree"

PAGE 21	
shiniest	brightest
swallow	get food down your throat and into your stomach
tummy	stomach, belly
bitten	cut with teeth
slice	piece
excited	happy
gulped	ate quickly
PAGE 22	
wailed	cried loudly
mistake	something you do wrong
promise	tell the truth
PAGE 23	
skin	outside of fruit
trick	fool; play a joke
warn	tell of danger
PAGE 24	
lie	something that is not true
PAGE 25	
takes a nap	sleeps for a little while
worry	get upset about something that might happen

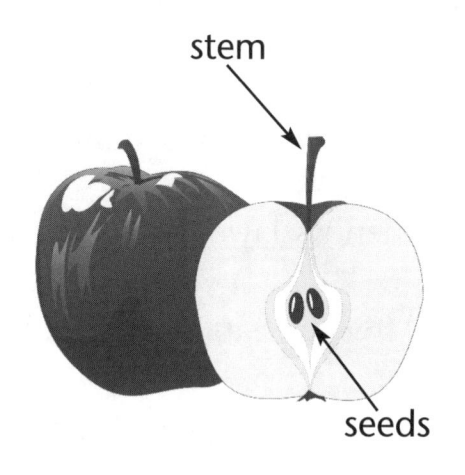

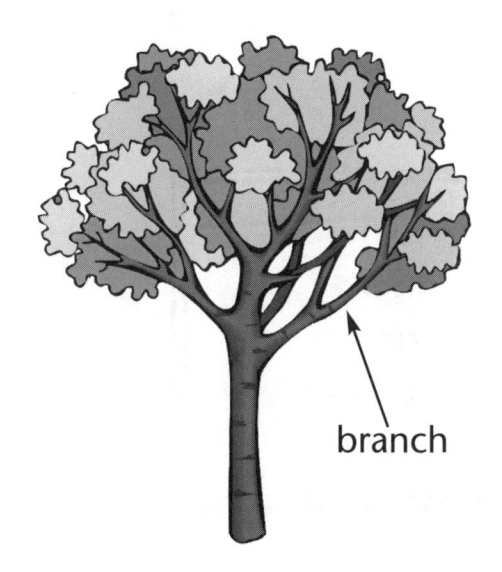

stem

seeds

oven

branch

Level B Glossary and Workbook: English 11

Word Mix-Up

Directions: The letters in the underlined words are mixed up. For each sentence, find the right word from the Word Bank. Write it in the blank next to the sentence. Number 1 is done for you.

1. Ellen picks the thiiesns apple. _____shiniest_____

2. Ellen wsslawol an apple seed. _____

3. After she eats the apple, Ellen's tymmu makes a noise. _____

4. Ellen's hafgnderatr bakes a pie. _____

5. Ellen's grandfather peels an apple. He takes off the apple's insk. _____

6. He puts the pie in the nove. _____

7. Ellen is txdeeci about eating some pie. _____

8. She ulgpde a slice down. _____

9. Ellen thinks a tree is gginrwo in her tummy. _____

10. She thinks that nacehrbs will grow out of her ears. _____

Word Bank

branches	oven
excited	shiniest
grandfather	skin
growing	swallows
gulped	tummy

12   AIM Higher! Reading Comprehension: Level B

✍ Writing Practice

Writing Prompt: Why does Ellen's tummy really hurt? Write your answer to the question on the lines below.

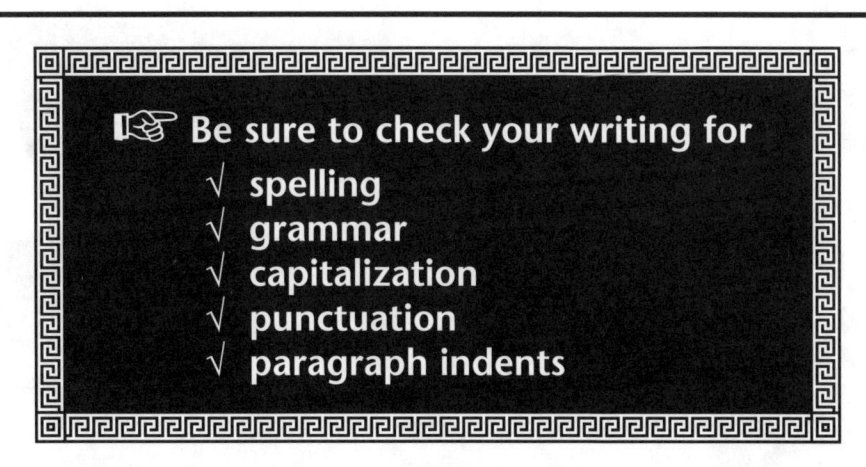

☞ **Be sure to check your writing for**
- √ **spelling**
- √ **grammar**
- √ **capitalization**
- √ **punctuation**
- √ **paragraph indents**

Level B Glossary and Workbook: English

"Give It a Spin"

PAGE 26	
string	piece of strong thread
tricks	fun things you can do with something
popular	liked by many people
earliest	oldest
painting	colored picture
clay	dried mud
soldiers	people in the army
carved	cut with a knife
PAGE 27	
looped	tied in a circle
middle	center
factory	building where things are made
space	where planets and stars are
PAGE 28	
curl	make wavy
PAGE 29	
law	rule you must follow
history	what happened in the past
PAGE 30	
vents	openings where air comes out

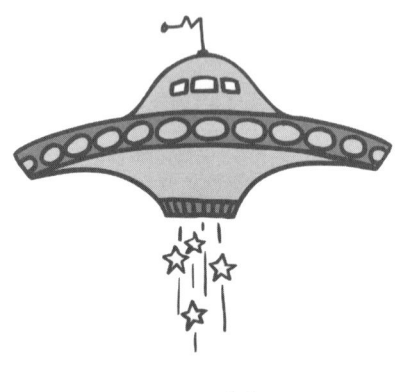

wrist

spaceship

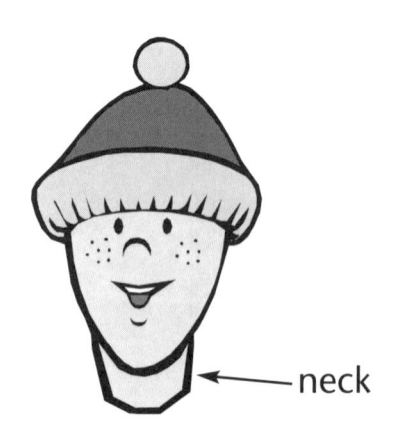

neck

computer

14 AIM Higher! Reading Comprehension: Level B

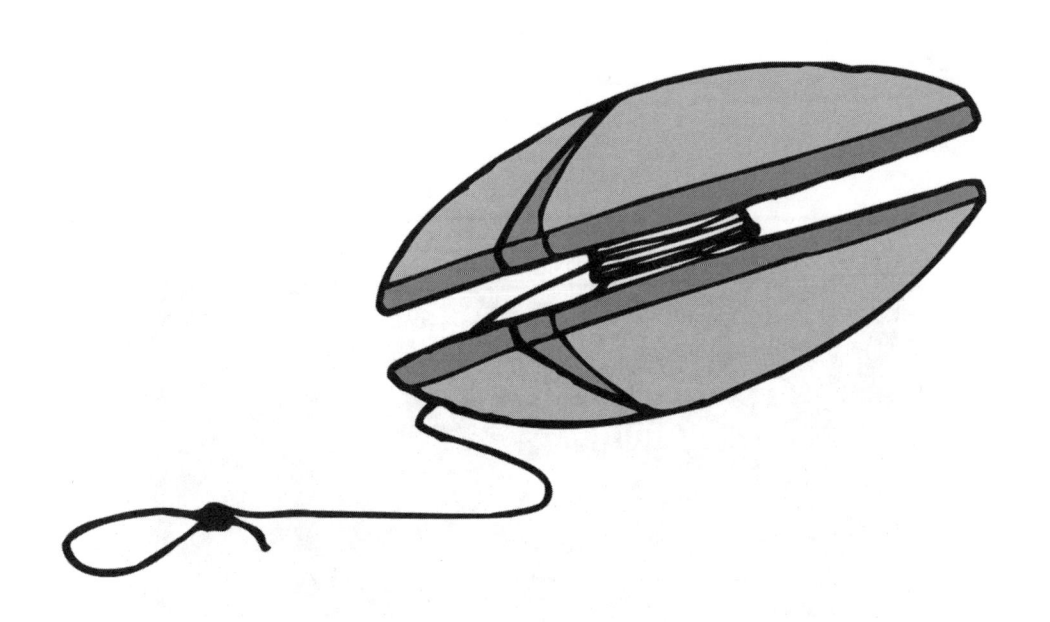

Secret Code

Directions: Each number stands for a letter. Write the letter above the number that it matches. Once the letters are filled in, you will see someone's name from "Give It a Spin." The first letter has been filled in for you.

Number-Letter Code:

1 = A	8 = H	15 = O	22 = V
2 = B	9 = I	16 = P	23 = W
3 = C	10 = J	17 = Q	24 = X
4 = D	11 = K	18 = R	25 = Y
5 = E	12 = L	19 = S	26 = Z
6 = F	13 = M	20 = T	
7 = G	14 = N	21 = U	

P __ __ __ __   __ __ __ __ __ __
16 5 4 18 15   6 12 15 18 5 19

✎ Writing Practice

Writing Prompt: Who was Pedro Flores? What did he do? Write your answer to the question on the lines below.

☞ **Be sure to check your writing for**
- √ spelling
- √ grammar
- √ capitalization
- √ punctuation
- √ paragraph indents

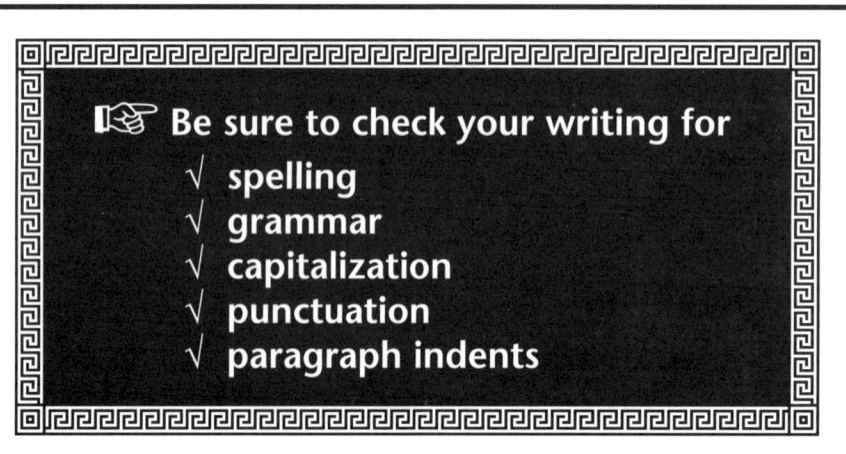

"Chasing"	
PAGE 31	
chasing	running after
caw, ruff, bzz	sounds that birds, dogs, and bees make
squawked	cried loudly
flew	went up in the air
yelled	called loudly
pet	an animal that you take care of at home
caught	taken and held
supper	dinner
PAGE 32	
tired	feeling sleepy
honey	sweet food bees make
sting	hurt with a sharp point

crow

clothes

Match the Picture

Directions: Write the letter of the correct picture next to the word.

1. ____ bee
2. ____ dog
3. ____ crow
4. ____ chase
5. ____ supper
6. ____ honey
7. ____ clothes
8. ____ sticks

a.
b.
c.
d.
e.
f.
g.
h.

Level B Glossary and Workbook: English   17

✍ Writing Practice

Writing Prompt: What game do you like to play with your friends? Tell why you like it. Write your answers on the lines below.

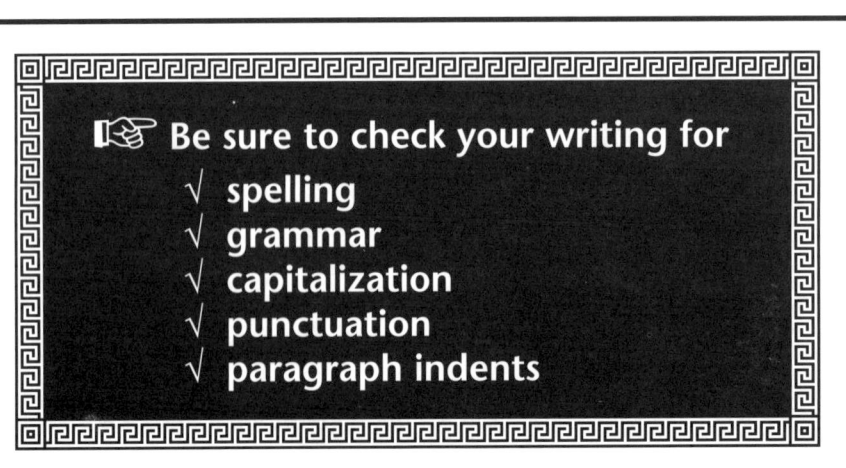

☞ **Be sure to check your writing for**
- √ spelling
- √ grammar
- √ capitalization
- √ punctuation
- √ paragraph indents

"The Ugly Duckling"

PAGE 35	
ugly	not pretty
fluffy	soft
PAGE 36	
autumn	fall
pond	small lake
weeds	wild plants that you don't pull out of your garden
thaw	melt
swan	big, white bird that swims and has a long neck
shore	land near water
pointed at	stuck fingers out toward
PAGE 37	
stormy	cloudy and rainy
PAGE 38	
forgets	does not remember
quack	make duck sounds

ducklings

nest

mirror

Level B Glossary and Workbook: English   19

Fill in the Blank

Directions: Which word fits in each sentence? For each sentence, pick the right word from the box and write it on the line. The first one is done for you.

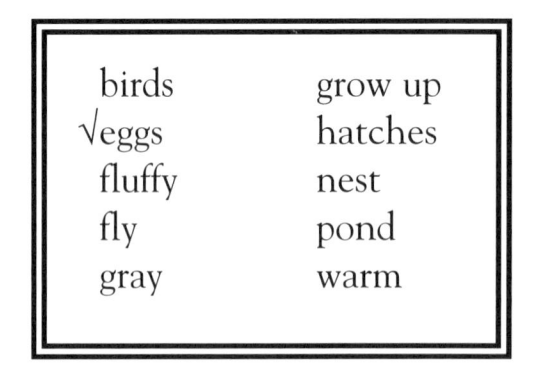

> birds   grow up
> ✓eggs   hatches
> fluffy   nest
> fly   pond
> gray   warm

1. A mama swan lays _____eggs_____.

2. She lays them in a _____.

3. When an egg _____, a baby swan comes out.

4. Baby swans' feathers are soft and _____.

5. Their feathers are _____, not white.

6. When they _____ _____, their feathers turn white.

7. Swans like to swim in a _____.

8. Their feathers keep them _____ when they swim in cold waters.

9. They also like to _____ in the air.

10. Swans are very pretty _____.

20   AIM Higher! Reading Comprehension: Level B

✎ Writing Practice

Writing Prompt: How do you think the Ugly Duckling felt when the other ducklings made fun of him? Write your answer to the question on the lines below.

☞ Be sure to check your writing for
- √ spelling
- √ grammar
- √ capitalization
- √ punctuation
- √ paragraph indents

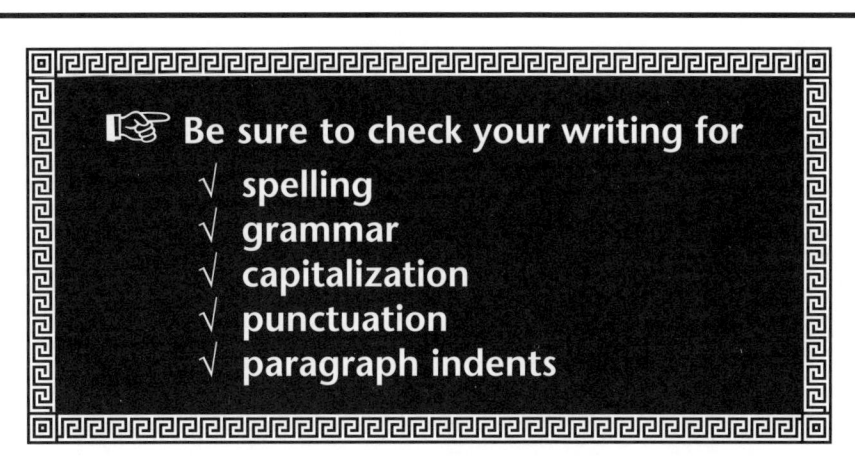

"Around the World in Twenty Days"

PAGE 40	
sail	use wind to move a boat
travel	go to other places
cabin	room hanging from a hot-air balloon for people to ride in
keep in touch with	talk to
team	group of people who work together
weather	how it is outside (cold, hot, snowy, rainy)
fresh	new, not spoiled
PAGE 41	
steered	made it move in the right direction
controls	instruments that let you steer
floated	moved slowly through the air
land	reach the ground
described	told about
moments	little bits of time
PAGE 43	
ran low	was almost gone
ran out of	had no more

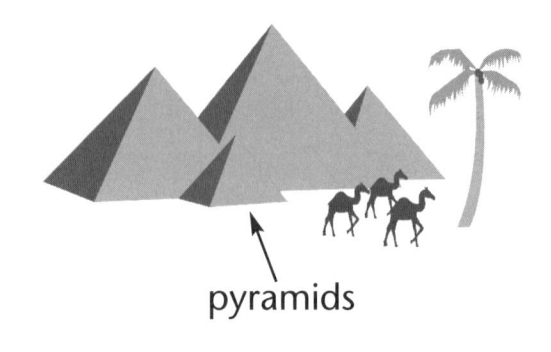

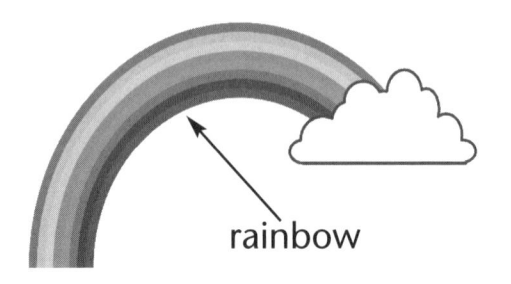

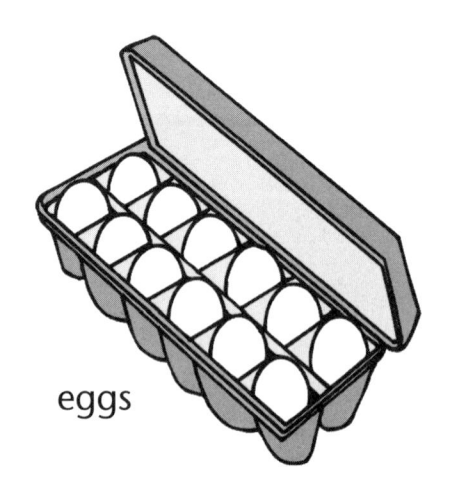

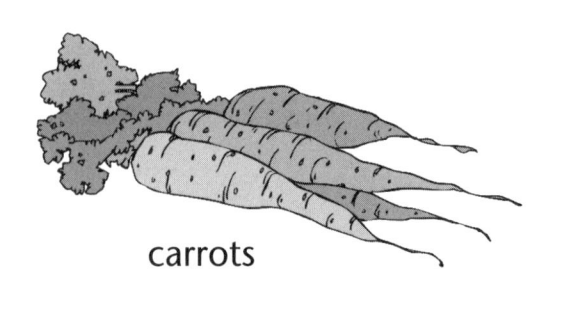

clouds

pyramids

rainbow

eggs

carrots

22 AIM Higher! Reading Comprehension: Level B

Word Whiz

Directions: Circle the correct word in each sentence below.

1. Letrice would like to (sale, sail) around the world.

2. The (whether, weather) is stormy and cold.

3. (Steer, Stear) the boat slowly.

4. Lin-mi likes to (travel, travil) to different cities.

5. The lily pad (floots, floats) on the pond.

6. Look at that pretty (rainbo, rainbow)!

7. Ms. Douglas lives in a (cabin, cabine) in the forest.

8. The fruit is (frech, fresh)?

9. The Fernandez family is going to see the (pyramids, piramids) in Egypt.

10. Mr. Getz asked Holly to (describe, describ) her new cat to the class.

Level B Glossary and Workbook: English

✍ Writing Practice

Writing Prompt: What foods did Bertrand Piccard and Brian Jones eat on their trip? Write your answer to the question on the lines below.

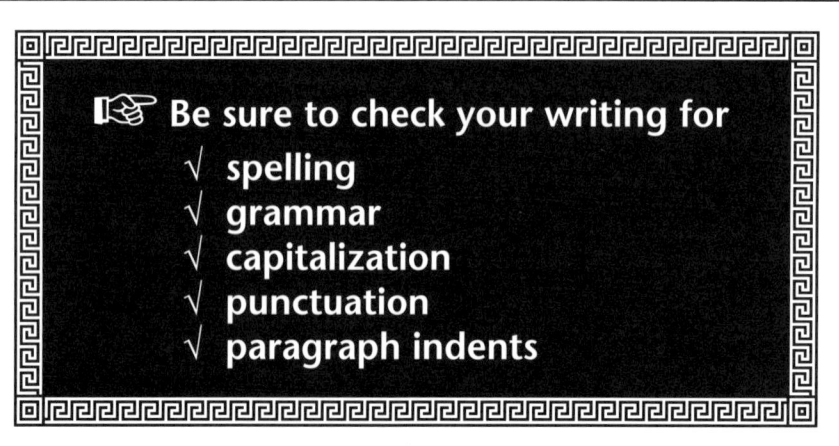

> **☞ Be sure to check your writing for**
> √ spelling
> √ grammar
> √ capitalization
> √ punctuation
> √ paragraph indents

24 AIM Higher! Reading Comprehension: Level B

"A Park Named Yellowstone"

PAGE 45	
national	of the whole country
wild	left to grow on its own, without people living there
waterfall	area where water rushes downward
forests	places with many trees and animals
beavers	brown animals with big teeth
streams	small rivers
bald eagles	strong brown and white birds
hot springs	hot water coming up from the ground
pool	small pond of water
reeled	pulled
PAGE 46	
faithful	dependable
shoots	sends something fast
boiling	very hot and bubbling
steam	gas from hot water
trust	know for sure
regular	always the same
PAGE 47	
underground	below the ground
PAGE 48	
sight	something you can look at
desert	hot, dry, sandy place
heats	makes hot
volcano	mountain that blows smoke

coyote

bighorn sheep

moose

apron

chef's hat

giraffe

mountain

Level B Glossary and Workbook: English

Crossword Puzzle

Directions: Put the word for each picture in the correct place in the crossword.

Across

2. animal with large horns

4. a _____ has big teeth

7. water rushed down a _____

9. a _____ is like a wolf

Down

1. this has leaves on it

3. a small river

5. a mountain that blows smoke

6. a _____ shoots steam

8. a _____ is hot and sandy

26 AIM Higher! Reading Comprehension: Level B

✍ Writing Practice

Writing Prompt: How did Old Faithful get its name? Write your answer to the question on the lines below.

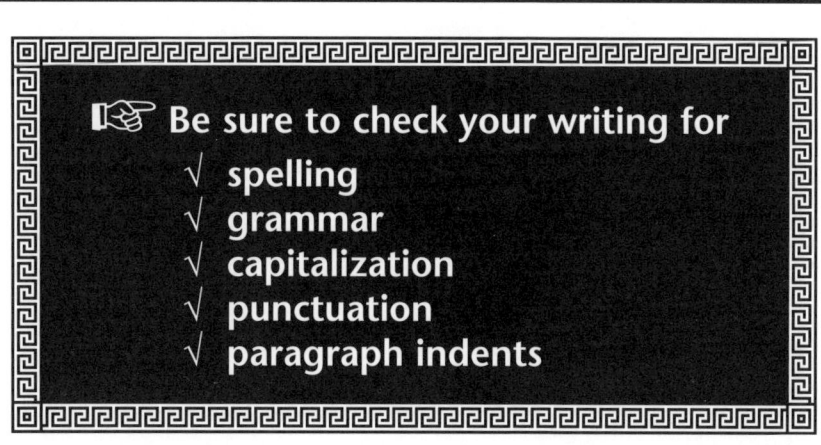

☞ Be sure to check your writing for
- √ spelling
- √ grammar
- √ capitalization
- √ punctuation
- √ paragraph indents

Level B Glossary and Workbook: English

"Up in the Sky"

PAGE 50

| bounces | comes back |
| closest | nearest |

PAGE 51

| rings | circles |
| sunrise | time when the sun comes up in the morning |

PAGE 52

| blocks | gets in the way of |
| crash into | hit |

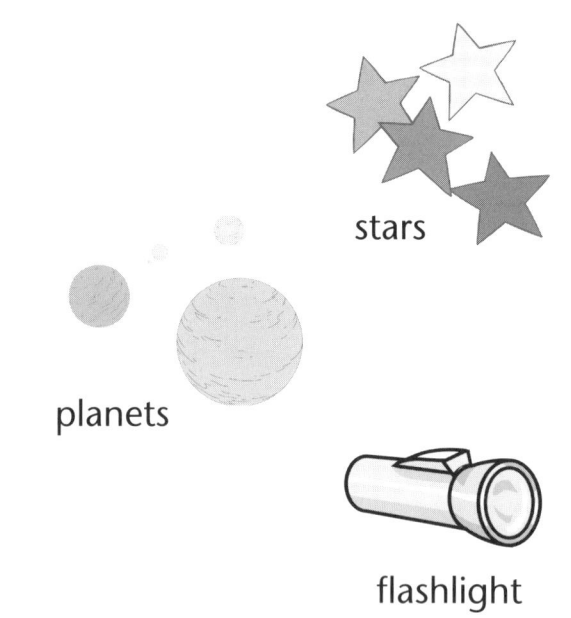

stars

planets

flashlight

Word Search

Directions: Find the words from the list in the puzzle below. The words go from up to down or left to right in the puzzle. When you find a word in the puzzle, circle it. The first word has been circled for you.

| √Earth | night | planet | Saturn | stars |
| moon | orbit | Pluto | solar | sun |

```
S  T  A  R  S  M  T  Z  I  S
A  A  P  C  O  H  K  M  Q  O
Q  G  L  F  L  S  V  X  A  P
S  P  A  E  A  R  T  H  R  E
A  L  N  O  R  B  R  Z  L  S
T  U  E  W  N  I  G  H  T  H
U  T  T  P  M  L  T  Y  W  N
R  O  D  P  O  I  O  S  W  N
N  S  U  N  O  R  B  I  T  E
Z  E  N  U  N  E  U  M  F  U
```

28   AIM Higher! Reading Comprehension: Level B

✎ Writing Practice

Writing Prompt: What are some interesting facts about the planets? Write your answer to the question on the lines below.

☞ Be sure to check your writing for
- √ spelling
- √ grammar
- √ capitalization
- √ punctuation
- √ paragraph indents

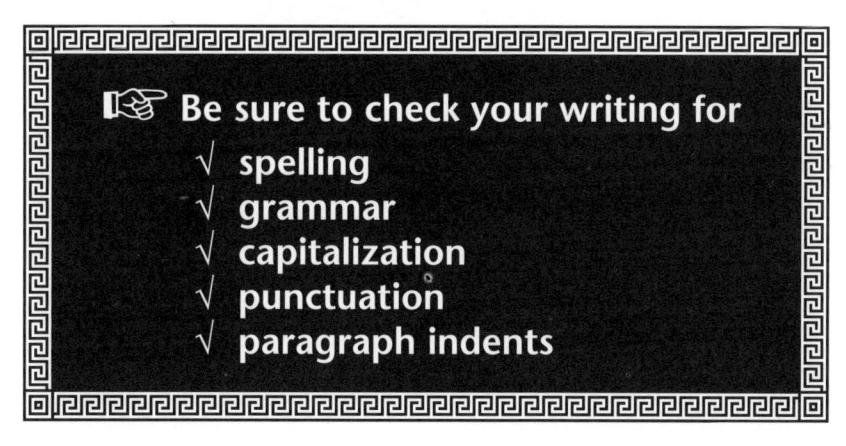

"White House Pets"

PAGE 55	
presidents	leaders of the United States
unusual	strange
pony	small horse
missed	felt sad without
elevator	machine that carries people up and down in a building
PAGE 56	
print	mark made by something
cart	small wagon
gates	parts of a fence that let people go in and out
favorite	what you like the most
melted	made hot and turned into liquid
statue	model of something
adopted	taken into a new family
Web site	information on the computer
PAGE 58	
cage	place where animals are kept
nickname	fun name to call someone
PAGE 59	
trick	joke

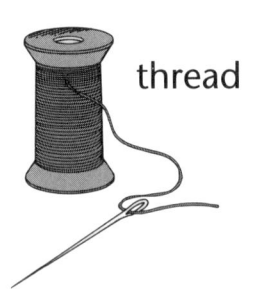

parrot

alligator

thread

goat

pennies

trash cans

newspaper

30　AIM Higher! Reading Comprehension: Level B

Whose Pet Is It?

Directions: Write the correct pet next to the president who owned it.

lion   zebra

silk worms   Polly

Socks   alligator

Yuki   Laddie Boy

Old Whiskers   pony

1. George and Martha Washington _____

2. John Quincy Adams _____ and _____

3. Theodore Roosevelt _____ and _____

4. Archie Roosevelt _____

5. Benjamin Harrison _____

6. Warren Harding _____

7. Lyndon Johnson _____

8. Bill Clinton _____

✎ Writing Practice

Writing Prompt: If you could have one of the pets in this story, which one would you choose? Why? Write your answers on the lines below.

☞ **Be sure to check your writing for**
 √ spelling
 √ grammar
 √ capitalization
 √ punctuation
 √ paragraph indents

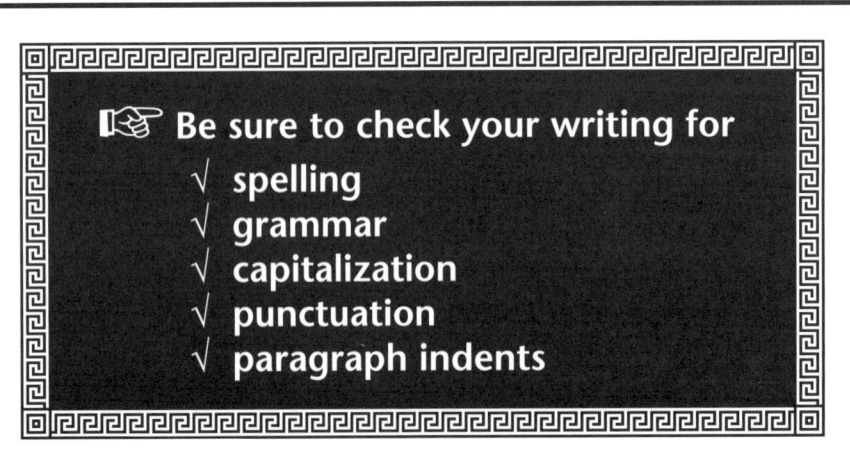